Zen in the Garden

Miki Sakamoto was born in 1950 in Kagoshima, Japan. She studied classical Japanese and Chinese literature in Tokyo and cultural anthropology (MA) in Munich, where she has lived since 1974. When living in Japan, she wrote for several newspapers. Alongside Japanese haikus and German poetry, she has authored works about Munich (*Münchener Freiheit* — Munich Freedom) and her grandmother (*Die Kirschblütenreise* — The Cherry Blossom Journey). Most recently she has written the poetic companion books *Eintauchen in den Wald* (Immersing Yourself in the Forest; Hanserblau, 2019) and *Zen und das Glück, im Garten zu arbeiten* (Aufbau, 2021) translated into English as *Zen in the Garden*. Last year *Lichtwechsel* (Changes in the Light), a volume of her poetry and nature writing, was published in German and Japanese (Weissbooks, 2021). She lives near Munich with her husband, the biologist and bestselling author Josef H. Reichholf.

Catherine Venner is a translator from German. She gained a BA from the University of Durham and a Master's from Europa Universität Viadrina. Her translations have been published in *World Literature Today*, *No Man's Land*, and the *Brixton Review of Books*. She lives in North East England and enjoys gardening.

Zen

in the

Garden

the Japanese art of
peaceful gardening

Miki Sakamoto

Translation by Catherine Venner

SCRIBE
Melbourne • London

Scribe Publications
2 John St, Clerkenwell, London, WC1N 2ES, United Kingdom
18–20 Edward St, Brunswick, Victoria 3056, Australia
3754 Pleasant Ave, Suite 100, Minneapolis, Minnesota 55409, USA

First published in German as *Zen und das Glück,
im Garten zu arbeiten* by Aufbau Verlag GmbH in 2021
Published in English by Scribe 2023

Every effort has been made to acknowledge and contact the copyright
holders for permission to reproduce material contained in this book.
Any copyright holders who have been inadvertently omitted from the
acknowledgements and credits should contact the publisher so that
omissions may be rectified in subsequent editions.

Typeset in Bembo by the publishers

Printed and bound in the UK by CPI Group (UK) Ltd,
Croydon CR0 4YY

Scribe is committed to the sustainable use of natural resources and
the use of paper products made responsibly from those resources.

978 1 914484 03 2 (UK edition)
978 1 957363 33 2 (US edition)
978 1 914484 03 2 (Australian edition)
978 1 761385 01 8 (ebook)

Catalogue records for this book are available from the
National Library of Australia and the British Library.

scribepublications.co.uk
scribepublications.com
scribepublications.com.au

Contents

III.

Preface

Throughout the year, and through the years, experiences and personal insights gained from my garden have created a collection of *niwa-yoku* moments — *niwa* meaning garden, and *yoku* meaning bathing. These experiences feature a cast of key participants: the plants and the animals. They are about the taste of home-grown tomatoes and problems growing cabbages, as well as dealings with potatoes, bugs, and caterpillars. The garden gives us moments of joy, reflected in quickly fading blossoms, enchanting butterflies, and the chirping of birds. Yet it also forces us to deal with aphids, snails, and grass mites without despairing or immediately and angrily attacking them with poison.

Niwa-yoku is how the Japanese describe the process of learning to be present with nature in our gardens. This approach uses garden work as a way to slow down, allowing us to inhale the aromas of the soil, and to attain a

1

state of meditative relaxation while working. *Shinrin-yoku*, which has become known as 'forest bathing', expands the perceptive horizon of our senses by actively removing all signs of the human world. In contrast, *niwa-yoku* narrows the horizon through immersion in a smaller world; one of shaping hands that follow the process of genesis and demise. *Niwa-yoku* understands nature as the creator and giver of life.

In *niwa-yoku*, the point of the Zen approach to gardening is not self-expression through gardening but rather the changes that the work creates in you. The fruits from the garden, the flowers, and even the landscaping of shrubs are not objectives that are set from the very beginning to be single-mindedly pursued; rather, they simply come into being as you work. The Zen approach allows you to accept what would otherwise be perceived as failure. It tells us that other living beings co-determine the genesis and demise of what is planted, and that they will shape the garden in their own way. Zen knows no pests; instead, it accepts them as collaborators and regards them as a reflection of the fruits of our endeavours.

Zen in the garden helps us to bring into focus the way we view things and helps us to centre our inner state. The result is an active, outwardly directed meditation that makes us more aware of the impact of our actions, and which can also become part of our philosophy of life.

My Garden

This book is largely about my, or rather our garden, which wraps around three sides of the house where we have lived for over ten years, ever since my hunsband and I decided to move to the countryside after decades in Munich. Our home's location in a 1970s housing development on the outskirts of a small town means that we have a generously sized garden by today's standards. The largest part, comprising roughly 250 square metres, stretches away from a patio attached to the south-west-facing end of the house, while a vegetable patch covering roughly sixty square metres can be found on the eastern side. They are linked by a broad passage to the south. Two sides of the property face on to streets, while the other two adjoin the neighbours' gardens.

The neighbourhood is quiet and residential, complete with traffic-calming measures. Trees grow everywhere,

3

and the view from the upper-floor windows is quite green, while woods stretch one kilometre east as the crow flies, bounded by an intensively farmed agricultural strip. Urban developments sprawl in all other directions. In short, it's an average location, typical of many suburban neighbourhoods.

Because it is only around fifty kilometres from the foothills of the Bavarian Alps, the town is guaranteed an abundance of rain, with an annual average of just under 1,000 millimetres. Our garden and the surrounding area, which is relatively low-lying at almost exactly 400 metres above sea level, is in one of the warmer regions of southern Bavaria. We still have hard frosts in the winter, but the cold is lessened by the *Föhn*, a warm Alpine wind that blows over us relatively often — luckily not as gustily as it does in Munich or the regions to the south of it. During my time in Munich, I really battled with the *Föhn*. Yet even there it brought conditions conducive to cultivating a garden, albeit a significantly smaller one.

The basic structure of both parts of our garden is easy to describe. The vegetable patch on the east side is nestled in the nook connecting the house to the garage, where it is bathed in morning sun and protected from the wind. The walls of the house store heat and release it overnight; grapes, as well as tomatoes, ripen particularly well nearby. In the winter, the wide borders generally stay snow-free and are warmed by the rays of the low sun. An impressive hedge of thuja, an evergreen conifer, lines the border with the neighbouring property to the east, while to the south, west, and north a high wooden fence shields the garden. In the front garden, thick bushes grow along the fence and merge into the hedge. A birch tree's double trunks and a very pointy pyramid of several thuja tower in the southeast section of the garden, and a ridge of hornbeams adds height on the north side. In the north-western corner sits a hexagonal gazebo, which I think of as my tea house. Open, pasture-like grass spreads away from it towards the patio, in front of which the star magnolia and buddleja bushes bloom.

Being in the garden feels like being on a secluded island. Over the course of the last decade, I have tried to intensify this effect. Even though we have nothing to fear in this neighbourhood, it's calming to know that the garden is essentially hidden from the outside. For as long as my dog lived and claimed it as his territory, this insularity was certainly a good thing. Maybe the blackbirds and robin redbreasts like it, too. I would like to think so.

This garden of roughly 350 square metres keeps me busy. My back tells me it is too big, but our blackbirds need an even larger territory than we can provide, and are forced to use the neighbouring gardens as well. It was ideal for my dog, though; he could rush around in it, burying things or doing his own 'gardening'. In emergencies, he used it as a toilet, but that was only when he was sick. Now, he is buried in it.

I try to cope with the demands of the garden, despite the protestations of my back. Many tasks make me feel meditative, but not all — some jobs are just too mundane and occasionally too frustrating. It is precisely in those moments that it does good to adopt a Zen perspective. Going into the garden every morning gives me strength. It is my counterpart in shaping genesis, growth, and demise.

Again and again, I observe what bliss it is to garden.

Chadō — The Way of Tea

A tea ceremony is only one of many possible ways of engaging with Zen Buddhism, but it is a special method, and requires a particular technique: *chadō*. This Japanese word means 'the way of tea', and it is closely connected to the garden. I understand *chadō* as the true and ideal path to finding yourself through practising the preparation of tea. Rikyū, the ancient master of the Japanese tea ceremony who lived between 1522 and 1591, gave this instruction: 'Heed what it means to bring water to a boil, to prepare the tea, and to drink it with a peaceful, contemplative heart in an upright position. This is a simple exercise, nothing more!'

The tea ceremony follows strict, ritualised rules. Each movement is considered an expression of your inner state.

Before entering a Japanese tea pavilion, you must wash your hands in a basin filled with fresh, clean water, conveniently located by a narrow entrance known as the *nijiri-guchi*. Its small size is to ensure that a samurai would have to remove his sword in order to enter. Weaponless and without haste, in one smooth motion, he would assume a sitting position, and then silently bow his head before a flower arrangement. The guest must bow before the flowers to express his devotion and emphasise his discipline. The tea is prepared in silence. Hot water is poured into a bowl containing tea powder, held by the drinker in both hands with devoted awe. In the moment of brewing, the shifting of the fingers, the flutter of a small cloth used as a serviette, and the barely perceptible movements of the upper body slow the flow of time until it appears to halt.

Harmony, respect, purity, and calm are central elements of the tea ceremony and its Zen philosophy. The tea bowls are perfected works of art, and the seasons dictate which ones are used. These bowls form part of the harmony of the pavilion, along with the flowers, the pattern of the kimonos, and the view from the opened sliding doors.

It is primarily women who become tea masters, although some men also practise for years to try to perfect the ritual of the ceremony. This devotion is not born of an obligation to better serve guests, but rather in the Zen belief that perfection, despite being unattainable, is worth striving for in its own right.

If I were in Japan, this belief would simply drive me towards the traditional tea ceremony. Only away from my homeland am I able to look at it afresh: the harmony that is striven for is not absolute, but can change depending on the situation. Sipping tea in my gazebo while observing the birds can create a peace comparable to receiving guests in a traditional Japanese tea pavilion. The journey to perfection requires practice, like playing a piece on the piano again and again. But immersing myself in a garden and its birdsong holds equal value, imparting a beauty that I can internalise.

'Practice makes perfect' is a common saying in Europe, an echo of the deep-seated desire to master certain skills that is so present in Japanese culture. However, mastery can be limiting; it can make people boastful. Tea master Rikyū warned against this. When a pupil asked him what the meaning of *chadō*, the way of tea, was, the master answered, 'Tea is nought but this: first you heat the water, then you make the tea. Then you drink it properly. That is all you need to know.' When the pupil replied, 'All that I know already,' Rikyū answered, 'Well, if there is anyone who knows it already, I shall be very pleased to become his pupil!'

These immortal words came to mind one day as I sipped tea and watched blackbirds and sparrows at the birdbath. Each one bathed in its own way, some more thoroughly and others just briefly. Clearly, they all had an eye on each other while bathing and behaved accordingly.

None of them were role models; all of them were copycats. I could imagine the blackbirds as Zen masters while the smaller birds, the pupils, watched their comings and goings. But even they did not set the rules. Every small life is lived for itself and is simultaneously bound to the lives of others, even including me as an observer and participant. My work in the garden has an effect on the birds, on all the other creatures that I admire or don't even notice because I pay too little attention to them, and on all the plants whose growth I encourage or prevent. When meditating, I become the centre because I make myself the centre. But all other living creatures remain their own centres. It is thanks to this insight that I value them, even the ones I do battle with.

The appreciation of mundane, trivial experiences forms a central aspect of Zen. Being entranced in meditation can be a means of escape from reality and its tedious demands. But the Zen mindset is one of embracing life, not fleeing from it. Zen neither focuses on achieving goals nor on avoiding fears, in this life or the next. The sparrows and blackbirds, the butterflies and beetles, the flowers and grasses, and all the other living things with which I come into contact tell me how much life itself is the answer. I only need to look at them, or even just sense them, and I no longer require any profound philosophy about the 'meaning' of life.

As everything moves towards its high point in the early summer, I experience life as far more than just myself. Time spent drinking tea in May or June conveys this feeling best, even though signs of decline are already evident. Spring flowers have withered and disappeared; I have to search for their remains to prove they ever existed. But I know that they will bloom again next spring, just as everything that symbolises summer is returning now, or will do soon.

In this I see another message: everything is changing, yet in changing it remains the same. Cycles, too many to comprehend, follow each other or occasionally overlap. But, just because there are a lot of visible changes happening at the same time in the summer, it does not mean that there aren't any happening in autumn or winter. Rather, it means that the rhythms of the cycles taking place are different or less obvious: they are ones that don't need long days and strong sun, like the cycles of early summer do.

I too need the sun, the long days, the warmth, and the feeling of things moving forward. It's the reason that the summer solstice makes me wistful. From then on, the year's glass is no longer still filling up; it will increasingly drain away until the turning point in the dark night of the winter solstice. Before then, I look forward to the weeks and months of harvest. First to appear are the strawberries, currants, raspberries, and lettuces; sweet and fresh with rich, distinct aromas. My garden calendar tells me summer is here when the tomatoes ripen. They are followed by cucumbers, pumpkins, kohlrabi, and, finally, apples, too. The buddleja will bloom, and we will watch butterflies and hoverflies flit around it in the sunny weather. Later, horseflies and wasps will plague us on the patio. The first yellow leaves will fall from the birch to the grass.

And, drinking my tea, I will know what I should do differently in the garden next year.

The garden will evade perfection — that is for sure. In Zen, there is no better, no more educational a sparring partner than gardening. The experiences gained from gardening solidify into an emotion that I call *niwa-yoku* in Japanese. In this book, I would like to show you a way to this state, a way that can lead to other paths to garden bliss.

I.

The Garden Through the Year

As trite as it may sound, I experience time differently in the garden. It is no longer divided into units of hours and days, or even months. It runs like a river, at times calm and at others rushing. I can assume that tomorrow will be very much like today, yet at the start of the year, all I know is that the coming twelve months will only roughly resemble the last twelve. And so, I plan my projects with provisos.

Many gardeners look forward to the new year with great anticipation. They can already imagine their handiwork in the form of vivid blooms and abundant fruits. I, too, start the year with the resolve to do some garden work, for you can't simply leave a garden to its own devices. Things would be very different were I to let nature take its course for even just a year.

Gardening is a task that is never quite finished. This is the basic lesson that every garden teaches. Constancy is an illusion and change is unavoidable. The more closely I observe what happens in my garden, the more aware I am of change. Its energy drives the plants' growth and demise, and creates the year's great cycle.

I better understand the essence of time while trying to resist change and, to a certain extent, when my expectations aren't met while gardening. For gardening is about what is yet to come but is not directly foreseeable. My goal could be something as simple as growing a lettuce to enjoy fresh from the garden, or harvesting the grapes that I hoped for when planting a sprig and cultivating it into a vine. The roses and hedge are pruned in the autumn because it will help make my visions of flowers in bloom a reality. I combat the aphids in May and June in order to enjoy the hibiscus flowers in July and August, and so on.

All this goes without saying, and I have always believed these observations to be unremarkable. However, over the years I have thought more and more about this 'implicitness'. Just as the Zen masters foretold, becoming absorbed in the processes of shaping the garden naturally develops into a sought-after emotion, a feeling you might pursue through meditation. Contemplation takes over as the objectives of the tasks become secondary; they should be unimportant, no matter how desirable strawberries, cabbages, or apples from your own garden may be.

If you focus too much on the harvest, you lose the profound meaning found in the present. The essence of being is crushed under the weight of your goals. 'The journey is the destination' is a phrase that has been overused almost to the point of meaninglessness, but it does effectively express what Zen is about. In my garden, the journey is the course of the seasons. It encompasses the changes in the garden that convey the passage of time, just as glancing at my watch tells me the hour or opening my diary reveals the date.

The cycles of the garden are different to the calendar seasons. There are no clear demarcations; the weather's variability, among other things, makes that impossible. I find that we cling far too tightly to clichés, particularly with weather, such as believing that winter brings blizzards, or that snow only falls in winter. The precise cycle of the astronomical year, upon which the weather bears absolutely no influence, does not draw a clear line between winter and spring, or other seasons. The only fixed points are the winter and summer solstices, and the spring and autumn equinoxes. However, nothing in my garden, nor out in the forests and meadows, offers any indication that even these fixed points are important markers for any natural processes. In this book, when I contemplate 'seasons' in relation to my garden, they are but a tool used to gain an overview. For everything is always in transition; nothing is definitively 'summer' or 'autumn', 'winter' or 'spring'.

I have never had any great difficulty in detaching myself from the notion of fixed seasons based on months or dates, because the seasons in my southern Japanese homeland are so different from those of Central Europe. The five periods of time that I use in reference to my garden instead are locally determined phases that demarcate the course of the year. They tell me a lot, and greatly determine what I consider doing in the garden and how I implement it. Above all, they illustrate the succession and merging of different life cycles. These phases teach me to respect the internal clocks of the various organisms I encounter while interacting with nature in the garden. As a result, my own sense of time encompasses a multitude of times, all flowing together. In this sense, I think the garden represents an open door with a view to the world beyond.

Ryokan hotels in Japan perfect the art of combining buildings with gardens. Throughout the seasons, they offer their guests a view of the passage of time through the ever-changing natural scenery that surrounds them. In Japanese haiku poetry, a so-called 'season character' indicates which phase of the year the poem relates to. The way I understand and experience the seasons largely corresponds with the Central European calendar. It also contains peculiarities that fascinate me or occupy my thoughts, but even if they are each allocated a season, the characteristics of each phase often don't fit easily into any wider pattern. Every 'walk through the gardening year' is idealised. I can't avoid that completely. Where possible, I try not to make my own perceptions of time the guiding theme. Experiencing garden time means detaching yourself from the calendar and the clock.

Slow Beginnings:
Spring

The seasons are out of sync. Every year, numerous people as well as the media confirm that this is in no way a personal prejudice stemming from my Far Eastern roots. Winter, with its snow and freezing temperatures, is expected in December. Its high point should come in January, bringing blizzards and hard frosts. February should see winter's end, and in March, spring is to begin. Yet February often brings the coldest temperatures of the year, and March, or sometimes even April, presents us with a covering of snow.

People say that it doesn't feel like Christmas without snow. And yet, over my decades of living in Germany, I have experienced snowfall from September to May, at the unlikeliest of times. This mistiming is not limited to the powdery white splendour; frost also makes untimely appearances. Long before my intense interest in gardening began, I gave up relying on the weather to indicate the season. Light is much more important to me. Grey

November days were not a feature of my childhood, nor were December weeks when it hardly ever gets light. Those days are simply too short. Every year, I hope for snowfall because it brightens these dark times. I imagine I am like a plant afflicted by the lack of light.

About three months after the bleak period of late autumn, the sun grows stronger and the days are finally long enough that the warble of a blue tit can be heard from the delicate branches of the birch in the garden each morning. It is then time to see how the snowdrops are getting on. Since the end of January, as the days have been getting milder, I have been waiting for the moment that their slender green tips pierce the last of the snow. What signals them to start growing? It remains a mystery to me. If it is the increasing length of the days, then their tips would poke through at roughly the same time every year. Could it be down to the temperature? We have seen Januarys that were milder than February or even March, and Januarys with heavy frosts that almost drove me to despair when I had to take the dog for early-morning walks and my breath froze in the air. But even in those years, a couple of days of the warm *Föhn* wind blowing over the garden at the start of February were enough for the snowdrops to begin peeping through the moss and the thin carpet of snow.

After a harsh frost, a great tit's song sounds particularly intense. I have even been rewarded with a greenfinch's warbling on those mornings when I would rather have

18

still been curled up in the warmth of my bed. The birds react to the dawn light and longer days — but what about the snowdrops? I have noted again and again that they are buried at least two hands deep in the earth and are also positioned in the shadow of the hedge. Do they have an internal clock, which last registered daylight sometime in late summer as their withered and browned leaves completely died back? It barely seems conceivable.

I have less difficulty figuring out the firebugs' life cycle. I see the first ones of the year in the ivy on the sun-bathed wall of the house. The unmistakable black-and-reddish-orange pattern on their backs looks threatening, and the poison in their bodies protects them from being eaten by birds, but they are harmless to humans. These oval-shaped bugs, approximately one centimetre long, have nothing to fear from me.

Their late-spring mating rituals are amusing. The males and females join the tips of their abdomens together with their heads facing in opposite directions. The semi-spherical male mounts the even more spherical female and holds that position for a while without any noticeable movement. The firebugs then run around while joined together. Very quickly, in fact. The female determines the direction, while the male runs backwards with her. I think this feat deserves some appreciation! By no means does the female move slowly, and yet the male doesn't simply allow himself to be dragged along.

For the time being, though, the firebugs are just sunning themselves on the house wall. On some days the sun awakens them, even if there is still some lingering frost. If the winter weather returns, they will retreat to the place in the earth where they hibernated. They avoid cold, wet weather, unhappy even when the temperature is five to ten degrees Celsius. I enjoy their reaction to the spring sunshine; it corresponds to my mood.

In the afternoon, winter crane flies often dance in the garden just as they do in late autumn and occasionally mid-winter, if there has been a strong *Föhn* wind that year. Snowdrops, dancing winter crane flies, and firebugs combine to form an early-spring trinity that unites passing moments with seasonality. The winter crane flies and firebugs react to the moment: the sun, the warmth from the *Föhn*, and the evaporating snow. The snowdrops remain even if a cold snap brings hard frosts and deep snow to the garden after the winter has supposedly passed.

Over the past decade, there have been such cold snaps nearly every year, especially if January and February were mild. This late winter clearly means nothing to the snowdrops and their cousins, spring snowflakes, which generally poke through five days after the snowdrops, but occasionally flower at the same time. These two beautifully named flowers sway in the spring wind, usually growing crowded together in small clumps; too crowded, I think. However, the snowdrops clearly have a different opinion, and a single cluster, small enough for me to encircle with both hands, can produce up to 180 flowers. It took me a couple of years to understand why they grow in this way. They multiply by producing offsets, or baby bulbs, from the parent bulb. Hence, my snowdrops are the clones of their ancestors. This is why they grow so densely, almost as if they have been squashed together, and why each plant in a single clump blooms more or less at the same time — they are all offsets from the same parent. These plants behave in the same way in the nearby riverine forest, their natural habitat.

In my garden I can see that some clumps have grown bigger over the years. I only rarely find individual new snowdrops somewhere on the lawn, where hundreds of them had flowered in the years before. When I do, I wonder: why aren't they vigorously multiplying there? Their flowers are eagerly visited by bees. Most years, they are already in bloom as the first honeybees emerge and fly from clump to clump, not just between flowers in the same crowd. That means there should be seeds, many seeds. Later in the year, when spring turns to early summer, I see the capsules in which the seeds are ripening. They rest on the ground or sag towards it, while the leaves of the snowdrops and spring snowflakes are still standing upright, lush and green.

In the nearby riverine forest they are much more evenly distributed than in my garden: their ripe seeds are spread by

21

ants. Each seed has a small oil- and protein-rich appendage called an elaiosome, which attracts the ants. Alpine squill seeds also attract ants, but for a long time the alpine squills in my garden were disappearing faster than I could plant them. And if the odd one miraculously survived, it looked pretty pathetic all on its own. In the local forest there are thousands of these blue squills growing in large, self-contained groups, or among the millions of snowdrops and spring snowflakes — come April there are always blue bands edging the pathways and swathes of blue sweeping over vast areas.

For a few years now, I have been more successful with the alpine squills in my garden, and new snowdrops and spring snowflakes have been popping up, too. I now know the reason: we had been mowing the lawn before the seeds had had time to ripen. The ants did not have time to collect and transport them to different locations. However, the existing bulbs survived, and each year formed bigger clumps of snowdrops or spring snowflakes with their offsets. Alpine squills are clearly not as good at producing offsets as snowflakes and snowdrops. They don't even form dense clumps in the wild. This is what comes to mind as I inspect my spring snowflakes on a crisp, sunny February day and note that the largest group has once again significantly increased. Maybe, in two or three weeks, it will put on a show of over 200 flowers. For now, all I can see is small white tips on dozens of green shoots.

I resolve to be more considerate of the spring flowers' seed formations when I mow the lawn. The enjoyment that they give me now and in the coming weeks is worth the extra care. But the plants don't die when their flowers fade: I notice with some shame that far too often I only pay attention to the flowers, as if they had been made for me rather than for insects or the snowdrop plants themselves.

Pondering this thought, I brush the last of the snow from the primroses that bloom under the rosebushes. Both varieties have bright, pale-yellow flowers, but are not related to the similar-looking cowslips that are found in the forests and meadows of Germany. The primroses are 'stemless', their petals sitting almost directly on top of a rosette of broad leaves. Over 250 years ago, Carolus Linnaeus named their parent species *Primula vulgaris*. They grow in the Atlantic climate zones of western and north-western Europe, and bloom throughout the winter. Their unseasonal flowering is due to the fact that their maritime region of origin doesn't experience prolonged frost and snow in winter. In late winter, the primulas already give me an indication of whether the plants in my garden have suffered from winter damage. They also reveal the potential benefits a layer of snow can bring, for it can actually protect the primulas and other tender, frost-sensitive plants in the garden; it acts as insulation, keeping the soil temperate and preventing frost damage.

Late frosts can be more dangerous for some plants, like tulips, especially if they have already developed buds. The condition the primulas are in acts as an especially good guide to the health of my roses. Most winters, I do not need to do anything to them after their autumn prune. However, their roots are at risk if icy but snowless nights are forecast, and they need to be protected in good time — especially when all the signs herald an early spring, but the nights are still longer than the days. Cold snaps can still occur after mid-March, when forsythias and almond trees are already in blossom.

I have the impression that early spring is the second-longest phase of the year, second only to the period of winter dormancy from November to February. As early spring drags on, sometimes very little changes in the garden for a full week. In the four, sometimes five tough weeks of early spring, I can prepare without distraction for the coming year. Then, slowly, life starts to awaken from the cold earth. The days become longer than the nights, and spring finally warms the soil. From the end of March, everything turns green and grows vigorously.

The calendar year starts much too formally on New Year's Day, with an excess of noise and the smell of burnt fireworks, the winter solstice having passed only a week and a half before. But I think that for the majority of people who live in regions with distinct seasons, the year only really begins with spring and the reawakening of nature.

The winter is to be endured. As soon as the sun has gained in power and height, things get noticeably better. Not only in the garden, but also in my body, which perceives the cycle of the seasons in this way, too.

In spring, by consciously observing what changes in the garden and what remains — at least externally — the same, I can prepare for the explosion of life that will arrive in April. Now, at the end of February, I am at leisure to watch two blue tits scramble about on the thin, downward-hanging branches of the birch. They investigate the tree's small, still tightly closed catkins. The hazel's catkins are already much bigger and longer. A couple of mild sunny days will be enough for them to extend fully and spread their pollen on the early-spring wind. Then, red styles will protrude, like tiny octopi, out of the full buds on the hazel branches; they are the female flowers. Discovering them gives me so much joy every year, not only because of the nuts they will produce, but also because of the way they catch drifting pollen with their small, spindly, stick-like arms. Unlike with grass pollen, I can gaze in awe at this mini miracle of propagation, as tree pollen does not cause my hay fever.

Later in the year, when the birch blooms, I am able to observe the blue tits' artistic gymnastics in silent amazement. They are so small, so delicate, and yet so cheery, as if delighted to be alive. It does me good to watch them; my sense of time is suspended, and everything else fades away. Only they exist: these small titmice with azure-blue caps, yellow breasts, and blue-grey backs. I wonder whether they are 'our pair', who nest each year in our birdbox and generally rear fledglings successfully, or whether they are winter visitors, who have arrived from the north-east and will fly back again in the spring.

Slowly my attention wanes. Once again appointments and obligations fill my head without invitation, replacing my reflections on the two blue tits. The soft warbling of a bullfinch takes me back to my worry-free observations for a few more moments. These larger, bulkier finches with their thick, conical beaks also perch on the birch and snap off buds. They usually consume them whole, but I notice that sometimes the firm brown husks fall off as their beaks close over them. The male is red; a strong scarlet covers his lower face to his breast. On the female, this part of the plumage is a pinkish-grey. It means the females are much less noticeable than the males, at least to humans, who can more easily recognise the colour red. The cats who roam the garden can't see the splash of colour — for them, red shades are just tones of grey, be it the blush red of a bullfinch or the orange red of a robin. If these birds hide under the hedge, they appear much like a greyish-brown mouse in the eyes of a cat.

The red-breasted bullfinches remind me of the robin I have been providing with specially prepared meals of oat flakes and hard-boiled eggs for the weeks since it started trying to overwinter in my garden. Out in the forest I only see robins on riverbanks, where wrens also linger. There, they can find small insects, spiders, and worms — but what can a robin survive on in my garden? It can't snap off any of the nutritious buds from the birch tree like the bullfinches and greenfinches, whose trilling song I hear almost every morning. A couple of years ago, I had to accept that although my food provisions can help, they cannot guarantee a bird's survival through the early-spring famine that frequently lasts so long. One March day, I found a robin lying dead at the side of the patio. I picked it up. It was light, far too light, just a little over ten grams, when it should have weighed fifteen to twenty grams. Its breastbone was poking out, its breast shrunken; it had starved. In December and January, I was sure that I had heard it singing in the bushes. When I finally heard a robin's song in the garden once more, it filled me with joy, and I hoped all the more for the arrival of true spring.

The next morning, I wake once again to the beautiful, piping warble of the bullfinch. Its call summons me barefoot into the garden. I take morning walks whenever possible, only skipping them when there is a hard frost. Today, with only a light frost sparkling white on the grass and roofs, the cold prickles my feet and perfectly stimulates my circulation. 'Peu, peu,' warble the bullfinches from the birch tree. 'See, see,' call the blue tits. 'Teacher, teacher,' or, 'tsee, tsee,' sing the great tits, while the sparrows chirp chaotically, an early-March hint of the oncoming spring dawn chorus. Collared doves join in with their monotonous, continual 'coo-cooo-cuck'.

With a start, I realise that I nearly stood on a daisy. It's not just the primulas that are flowering, as they would in their wild Atlantic homelands, but 'our' daisies are also beginning to bloom. This year, these small plants are the first to unfold their glory, even before the snowdrops. But have they only just flowered, or have I missed them in recent weeks due to the ground frost and a layer of snow? This question takes on a momentary urgency. I'm sure that they were still flowering in December, after Christmas. But what has happened to them since? Are the flowers I noticed today new or old, from this year or last? The question is of no importance to the life of a daisy. They flower when the conditions allow it. I notice them in late autumn when the other plants have retreated into winter dormancy or have died off. And I see daisies again in early spring when other vegetation has not yet sprouted and overgrown the tiny plants. These multi-petalled white stars with yellow centres bloom most magnificently after the lawn has been mowed, littering the grass as if scattered by children.

They are always there, these small daisies, but I usually overlook them because my attention is focused on other things. I discovered their scientific name in the plant encyclopaedia; it lovingly describes them as *Bellis perennis*, or 'eternal beauties', as my husband translated for me. Beautiful, year in, year out: what praise indeed for the tiny daisy! My husband also told me that young girls make crowns of daisies to put on their heads, or wear on their wrists like bracelets. As a child in Japan, I did the same with white clover flowers. Apparently, domestic geese like to eat daisies, which may have contributed to their name in German, *Gänseblümchen*, which translates to 'goose flower'. I once saw this for myself as I watched a young greylag goose at a quarry pond. A fluffy yellow gosling, which still wobbled cutely as it walked, plucked purposefully at the daisy flowers growing in their thousands on the banks of the pond.

As I look at the frost-covered daisy next to my big toe on this early-spring morning, which holds the promise of a beautiful day, it's strange what comes to mind. Images follow one after another as I look from the birch to the forsythia and inspect their buds, then turn my attention to the camellia, which is enjoying the protection of a reed mat that I have wrapped around it. Its plump buds look much more robust than those on the forsythia, but they are actually a great deal more tender. I have to protect them if I want to admire their flowers, which open like red roses in April. I also glance at a nearby pile of leaves in the hope that the hedgehog hibernating under it is doing well. It's possible — probable, even — that there are mice hiding in the pile as well. On gloomy winter evenings, I saw them climbing up the shrubs to get at the bird-feeding station, their big ears and long tails revealing them to be wood mice rather than the voles I am not as keen on having in the garden.

In spring I get up late and go into the garden at precisely the time that the rising sun casts the birch branches' shadows like lace over the frosted earth. They look like a huge ink painting on textured, tissue-thin paper. Admiring this delicate image makes time stand still for more than just an instant. At this moment, something that can only roughly be described by the term 'Zen' takes hold. In the morning tranquillity, silence reigns.

Only rarely, when all the conditions are right, does such a moment exist. From experience, I know that it is better not to search for them; they must be allowed to happen naturally. The effect is more intense without any prior effort. A picture painted by light isn't the only thing that can transport me. A robin's softly rolling song, or even the smell of freshly dug compost, ready to be spread around my flower beds, can also carry me off.

My eyes might notice a multitude of tiny creatures bustling about in the compost, but what goes to my head, literally through my nose, leaves a much stronger impression. For minutes, this breath, taken from the earth, seems to move my hands without me having to steer them. It is only when some compost worms, blue-red and chubby, move in the shimmering, black-blue humus that my thoughts return, my awareness of a robin and his song. I step back, take the bucket of fresh earth, and go to the flower beds, thinking: now the robin can forage in the humus of the compost.

Or perhaps my thoughts return to the blackbirds, who are no longer simply sitting, motionless, with their feathers puffed up, as in winter. A few of them have reclaimed my garden as their territory and begun to defend it against other blackbirds. The male sings early in the mornings from the pavilion or the birch, depending on whether it is windy and his song needs protection from the gusts. He is chased back and forth through the garden by the brown female. Her beak is somewhat yellow, not as orange as the male's, but it still shows her age and strength.

If I watch the pair for a while, I get the impression that she is the one who makes the decisions, not the magnificent, velvety-black male who sings so captivatingly. His songs are loud, demanding, and repellent at the same time. I like hearing them, above all now, in early spring. But they don't move me in the same way the languid trills of the robin do. In their daily lives, and even when they sing, neither species violates the other's turf. I want to have both in the garden throughout the summer, year after year, but only the blackbirds stay. The robins don't have a chance. Far too often, death is lurking in the hedge.

For the robins, the winter months are safer than the spring. Cats stay at home or go outside only briefly and generally during the day, when they are easily spotted by

31

the robins. But the longer the days become, the later the cats roam. Despite being colour-blind, they can see much better than robins can. In low light they can even see better than humans.

When my dog was still alive, I often thought of leaving him outside overnight. He would have easily kept the garden free of cats, but the indiscreet 'commentary' he would have kept up throughout the night prevented me. During the day, he protected the birds, but at night the robins had to look after themselves. Blackbirds, titmice, finches, and pigeons can find cat-safe sleeping and nesting sites in the trees, but ground-nesting robins cannot do this. Sticking to the parts of the hedge that are particularly thick on the ground is not always enough to keep them safe. In early spring, when day and night grow closer in length, the robins disappear.

I make a small discovery in the compost that gives me a jolt: a clutch of slug's eggs. But then I notice that the eggs are flat, as if they have gone too soft; they have perished. Truthfully, I can't live in peace with slugs, those large, brown, slimy creatures whose scientific name, *Arion*, sounds far too nice in my opinion. I even find the German word *Nacktschnecke* — literally meaning 'naked snail' — unsuitable. I would rather not think about them at all. Many people believe that a winter with little snow but prolonged yet light night frosts will decimate the hibernating slug population. I affirm this hope with a sigh.

I will only know more in May, when the customary rainy period, or 'slug weather', sets in.

I see a dry May as invaluable, and also very beautiful. I know that the forestry and agriculture industries hold a different opinion, but as much as they would appreciate their ideal showery weather, I don't want it. I flinch at my straying thoughts. They are not congenial to the serenity that working in the garden usually helps me achieve. I try to distract myself with the question of whether the Zen masters ever had to combat slugs. Unfortunately, I can't think of any ancient teachings about them doing so. Maybe they saw the slugs as a good example of the success to be had from slow perseverance.

A brown leaf whirls through the garden, horizontally at first, and then rising upwards. The next minute, I realise that it is actually a butterfly, with small tortoiseshell wings. It is the first butterfly I've seen in the garden this year. The southerly *Föhn* wind will probably have carried it over the Alpine foothills from the mountains to here. It flies on, without taking even a single turn around the garden. In March, the small tortoiseshells often migrate in large numbers from Italy and Croatia northwards over the Alps. They follow the river valleys that lead to the Danube, using the *Föhn* as a tailwind. For many years, my husband and I studied the migration of butterflies on the River Isar close to Munich. It fills me with joy that one of them is now flying through my garden.

Brimstones are usually the first butterflies of spring. They hibernate here in Germany, sometimes even in gardens as well as the country's forests. I see them in autumn, the vibrant-yellow males and the pale-yellow or ivory-coloured females, searching for a suitable place to overwinter. No matter how much I want them to, they never settle in my garden. I only know what they look like during their winter sleep because of photos taken by friends. The hibernating butterflies hang in the undergrowth with their wings pointing downwards, like a pale leaf hanging still on a branch. If a frost follows a damp winter evening, they will be covered in icy needles of frost. They can survive up to minus twenty degrees Celsius in this exposed position because their bodies contain a natural antifreeze, meaning that no ice forms inside them. Early spring reawakens them to life, and the males fly tirelessly along the paths and edges of the forest, until the females also wake up days or weeks later.

When I eventually get around to planting a couple of alder buckthorns, the females will lay their eggs on them, and caterpillars will eat the young leaves, pupate, and then hatch as fresh brimstones in late June or July. The males will court the pale-yellow females in an air dance. And I will enjoy watching them from the patio, with a cup of tea in my hand, warmed by the April sun. Of course, I will plant the buckthorns ... someday. There are so many things that I have planned to do, and the deeper I delve into the life of my garden, the more tasks I discover. It's ongoing work.

Satisfied, I watch the snowdrops and spring snowflakes, their flowers gently swaying, although I can't feel any breeze. Next to the hazel bush, the small spring crocuses are opening their pale-lilac petals. They will be followed by much larger ones in saffron yellow and dark purple. Although I know when to expect them, every year their sudden appearance surprises me. It still feels as though their delicate light-blue or yellow tips shoot up through the moss without warning, and within the next day or two I already have fully opened crocus flowers. They are, of course, accompanied by bees, who crawl into their chalice-like blooms and get down to business.

But now, like almost every other year, there is a setback in the form of a cold snap. We have to get through it, the garden and I. Sometimes you also get such weather in April or May, other times it doesn't come at all and the garden blooms and grows — a real delight. However, I dare not even hope for that because I have been disappointed so many times. Consequently, I am all the more careful in making sure that no late frost scorches the camellia or the unfolding flowers of the star magnolia.

For me, the magnolia's white petals harbour the magic of spring. The beauty of the snowdrop is subtle, but a star magnolia laden with flowers is such an extravagant sight that when I look out of my bedroom window in the early mornings and see its magnificence, I want to bow in front of it, a remnant of my Japanese upbringing. When the weather is sunny, cool, and dry, the flowers can last for a good week, and in some years almost two, before the gradual growth of the leaves emerges through the white stars, turning the tree's branches pale green. Then the narrow petals, almost as long as a little finger, fall to the ground, forming a large wreath around the bush. Even this phase, which only lasts a few days, fascinates me. Only when the petals start to turn brown do I admit that the time of the star magnolia is once again over.

The star magnolia fits well in my small garden. I use it as a replacement for Japan's iconic cherry blossoms. Of course, there are also ornamental cherries here in Germany. But I don't want to create small-scale, reflected glory. I could never cultivate enough trees to create the profound effect of the *sakura* of Japan. There is not enough space or structure to the landscape. For me, cherry blossom should remain synonymous with my homeland.

When the blooming of the star magnolia overlaps with the flowering period of the forsythia, as is usual in my garden, I barely look at the latter's bright-yellow blooms. Their flowers promise too much, deceiving the bees and other insects attracted to the neon yellow, because they provide nothing for them: the forsythias in my garden are artificially cultivated hybrids whose flowers are sterile. The bees' efforts are in vain, and each year they must be disappointed.

For a long time, I was unaware of this, and now I know, I wonder whether it is right to cultivate this yellow splendour when all it gratifies are our eyes. Even once the flowers have withered, the forsythia offers the insects and birds next to nothing. At most, blackbirds can build nests among its compactly pruned branches. In gardens and parks, many things are only for show; they are created to provide an impression of the seasons.

For humans, the start of spring is heralded by forsythia, but for bees, this message is better transmitted by a goat willow's flowering catkins. It is just as necessary to place a sign saying 'a bee-friendly willow grows here' next to blossoming willows as it is to display a sign saying 'a flower meadow grows here' to prevent over-eager maintenance workers from mowing everything down as soon as the first flowers unfold. Apparently, flowers equate to untidiness, especially for council workers policing road verges. At best, only a flower bed sown by humans will be spared. When spring arrives and nature gains momentum, the destruction begins. It's really depressing.

As lawnmowers drone on, and in many gardens the grass is cut so short that not even daisies survive, my garden becomes an island to which I can retreat. Right now, in spring, there is something new to discover almost every day. The common field-speedwell, to be precise, has started flowering. Up close, its delicate petals look like a reflection of the sky, with white cloudy wisps against pale blue. The bugle is also coming, pushing its stems upwards; it will soon create a swathe of deep blue as its flowers open. Of course, I have tulips in the garden. They range in colour from white with fringed petals to almost ink black. Yellow daffodils bloom consistently, and not just around Easter, the celebration with which they are synonymous.

From the flight direction of the bees, I can tell that my currant and raspberry bushes have also come into bloom. Their flowers are inconspicuous, the complete opposite of the flamboyant tulips, which, after flowering, don't leave anything behind but leaves that grow paler and sallower with time, as if decaying. The barely noticeable berry flowers turn into delicious red- and blackcurrants in June, and the raspberry bushes produce berries for months.

If I were to categorise spring flowers according to their conspicuousness, I would say that the more noticeable they are, the less abundant they tend to be. Apple blossom, however, is an exception to this rule. The flowers are very beautiful, possessing a rose-like allure. When the blossoms come into their own at the end of April or the start of May, it is definitely a sign that a good apple harvest will follow. And if a late frost or hail should prevent that, it will not have been due to a lack of promise on the flowers' part.

With the exception of apple blossom, my observation is correct — the really glorious flowers tend to be less prolific and productive, even the roses. None of my best-looking roses give me rosehips, and some are not even that attractive to bees, no matter how wonderful I think they look. The bees and rose chafers prefer the small-flowered, open roses that provide more pollen and an enticing scent.

For me, apple blossom signals the end of springtime. From the end of April, the long, almost leisurely awakening of the new year is over. April does justice to the Latin word it is derived from (*aperire*, 'to open'), and throws open the earth's bedchamber, allowing a plenitude of nature to escape. The hesitation is over, and time is pressing. Flora and fauna can no longer afford to be hesitant. In just two months, the year will reach its high point: the summer solstice. The outcome of the year depends upon these two pivotal months.

It would all be fine if it weren't for the weather. There are often setbacks with the weather in May. This supposedly 'wonderful' month is usually cold, damp, and unpleasant. I dare not think of how rarely we have enjoyed good May weather in the last thirty years. But May and June barely permit any time for contemplative observations, anyway. Action is needed; the garden tells me so day after day.

Towards the High Point:
Early Summer

Now the garden's growth is approaching its high point so quickly that I can barely keep up. Major dramas are unfolding concurrently: lettuce vs snails, cabbage vs caterpillars, and flowers vs greenflies. In all three cases, I am involved in battles that are not conducive to tranquil meditation. They rank among a gardener's worst problems and make me feel as though I'm constantly on the verge of failure.

I would despair, were it not for all the splendour that appears of its own accord, establishing itself without my help. Peonies are a great example; their palmate leaves emerge and grow bigger and bigger until fist-like hemispheres form between them. The buds swell up, turning from green to pale pink, and bursting open when they believe it to be Pentecost. They become so large and heavy that a light rain shower is enough to make them sag to the ground. The pink foam-like balls are too big for a traditional Japanese *ikebana* bouquet. They look glorious out in the garden, just a few metres from my Japanese acers.

Some hydrangeas would also look good by the small acers, but my currant bushes are already growing next to them, the inconspicuous flowers having been visited intensively by bees and other pollinators. The redcurrants ripen before the summer solstice, but the exceptionally aromatic blackcurrants need a little longer, often taking until July.

In the hedge surrounding the garden, the roses, privet, dogwood, weigelas, and mock orange are in bloom. The mountain ash and privet blossom are extremely fragrant; humans don't particularly like the smell, but the scent is especially attractive to bees, beetles, and flies. They are at least as enticed by these blossoms as I am by roses, which provide me with splendid flowers from the end of May onwards, despite — or maybe because of — my heavy pruning. No matter what the weather does, my roses bloom in front of the window right into winter.

Out on the lawn, thick green stalks grow to knee height, form a flat bud, and open up into palm-sized stars: marguerites. Irritatingly, colonies of black aphids occasionally form on the stalks right under the flowers. Are they in league with the masses of aphids on the hibiscus bushes? Are they rivals, or do they aid and abet them? Finding a ladybird on a marguerite flower normally means that I should take a look under the petals. I can easily squish the pests that sit on the smooth stalks with my fingers, but it is, of course, unpleasant. I cannot remember ever seeing aphids out on the street embankments where large groups of marguerites grow. Most likely, I simply did not notice them, as I only viewed the flowers from above.

May and June are my favourite time to sit in the gazebo, looking out into the garden through the open windows and the door. The blackbirds hop about, search for food, and sunbathe. If the sparrows splash around in the birdbath, then the blackbirds watch for a while as if deciding whether to go into the water themselves. Bathing is a group activity for the sparrows; if one of them starts, the others join in. Collared doves scuttle about nearby, bobbing their heads, but they are clearly uninterested in a bath. When a green woodpecker also appears, poking around in the lawn for ants or beetle larvae, I can barely concentrate on the book I picked up to read. I give up and watch. Tea suits this moment perfectly. Without taking my eyes off the busy birds, I bring my cup slowly to my mouth, and take a drink so small that it's no more than a sip.

Summer

The calendar states that summer starts in July, but according to the sun it starts on the day of the summer solstice. The shortening days act as a signal to nature to adjust its clock. The blackcap that has been singing constantly since April appears to tire. His songs are shorter now, more rarely heard, and no longer as full of intensity. From the beginning of July, the periods in which I don't hear any birdsong increase. The German poet Gottfried Benn encapsulated this time perfectly with the line, 'Never lonelier than in August'. Even the swifts, zigzagging over the garden hunting insects invisible to the human eye, refrain from calling out to one another as much.

Black swifts are becoming rarer from one year to the next. I have been following their decline for a decade. The few who make it to our small town are late arrivals, generally coming in the second week of May. Yet, they should be arriving earlier on account of global warming. Strange. In Munich, there were a lot more swifts, hunting insects over the district where we lived.

My garden is much too small truly to help boost the number of small insects in the air. Were I not to feed the sparrows all through the summer, I would most likely no longer see any of them in my garden. Only the blackbirds have it better. They benefit from lawn mowing; it keeps the earth and its worms accessible to them. Even so, they still don't fare very well. Not only do their broods fall victim to cats and magpies, but a few years ago, an epidemic decimated blackbird populations. Mosquitoes transmitted the Usutu virus, named after the river in South Africa where it was first detected, and, unfortunately, the disease keeps resurfacing.

When 'my' blackbird, whom I'd named Emma, died in 2019, I had no idea that just one year later a viral pandemic would plague humans, too — although the mortality rate of COVID-19 is much lower than that of the blackbirds' Usutu virus. During the COVID-19 pandemic, many people found respite in their gardens. Those who had outdoor space ranked among the privileged, even if it was just a few plant pots on a balcony. Confined to our homes and forced to take 'staycations' instead of travelling, many rediscovered the joys of a garden, learning that they had more to offer than simply providing the setting for a barbecue.

In the days around the summer solstice, I often feel noticeably melancholy: it's downhill from then on. But the feeling dissipates when I catch sight of the morning glory's buds in the early sunlight, their trumpets catching my eye as they reach towards me. When I look more closely, everything around them blurs, and I feel like I am being sucked into their depths. The bumblebees seem to feel the same way, as they disappear into them early in the morning. When they re-emerge from the velvety lilac-red flowers, pollen clings to their bodies and is carried to the next flower, and then the next.

The flowers' English name, morning glory, is more apt than their German name, *Prunkwinde* or *Prachtwinde*, which both translate to 'winds of pomp'. These names do not suit these flowers, which I don't find at all pompous. An unusual characteristic of the morning glory is that its flowers open early in the day; by midday, the edges of its trumpets are already beginning to curl up, and by the afternoon the flowers are completely withered. Like the field poppy with its silky-soft, blood-red petals, the morning glory blooms with flower after flower, but only in the morning hours with its head directed towards the sun.

In contrast to the poppy, which exhausts its power reserves over a few days in early summer, the morning glory continues to flower into autumn. For that reason, I regard this plant as a symbol of summer. Growing, climbing, and stretching, always reaching towards the light of the morning sun, training it presents a small challenge. With a trellis of the kind used for climbing roses, and string strong enough to withstand summer rain and storms, I guide it in the direction of my choice. In the process, its huge, heart-shaped leaves become dynamic sculptures, growing wherever I direct their soft, greenish-yellow tips.

In the autumn, the morning glory produces hundreds of golden-brown seed capsules. I always collect a couple of dozen to sow the next year. Sometimes, I note down what colour they are: pale pink, lilac red, sky blue, or dark, deep blue. I like to grow all four, because in the early-morning light they each glow in their own particular way. They are easy to start off; they grow without the need for special soil, fertiliser, or much care. Their only requirement is that they face the morning sun.

Thirty, fifty, or even more trumpets may open up in a single summer morning, all straining out of the lush blue-green foliage towards the early light. Watching them, I am as happy as I was as a child in our garden in Japan, where morning glory also bloomed. It grew around our east-facing kitchen window. I sometimes think of doing an experiment to see if the morning glory flowers could be planted in the shape of a Japanese flag: a red rising sun in a white field. What could be more appropriate?

As a child, the leaves of the morning glory cast shadows on our kitchen window, which we appreciated because the sun is very strong in the far south of Japan — more or less on the same latitude as the Nile Delta. I found the subdued, greenish morning light that shone into the kitchen soothing. We generally avoided the sun as much as possible; it shone excessively until the monsoon season started. Then light turned to warmth, creating a heavy, sometimes oppressive heat. I never encountered sunbathing until I moved to Europe.

Here, it nearly always takes too long for early spring to become full spring, and for early summer to become high summer. Cold spells in June make me shiver, while days or even weeks of rain in July drive me to despair. Comforting warmth often only arrives late in the summer, giving us Mediterranean-feeling evenings to enjoy outside on the patio. If a summer day starts with rain, the already-open flowers of the morning glory hang obliquely downwards. I cannot experience this as anything but an expression of sadness, even though the petals look entirely enchanting when raindrops trickle from them. If the droplets reflect the morning light, I allow myself to hope that the rain will stop.

This plant, which bears the scientific name *Ipomoea violacea* (or *Ipomoea tricolor*), holds a very special significance to the Japanese; it was one of the first plants to begin flowering again in soil contaminated by the nuclear bombs dropped on Hiroshima and Nagasaki. In doing so, it became a sign of hope. Those events are now so long ago that only a few survivors remain to remember them. But I can see for myself year on year what these plants can actually withstand.

Here, I am not just talking about my morning glory, but also its close relative, the field bindweed (*Convolvulus arvensis*). Its flowers are much smaller, only two to three centimetres long, and pale pink, while its leaves are narrow and arrow-shaped. Field bindweed creeps along the ground until it reaches a stalk and climbs up it, sometimes to above knee height. Then, it turns its petal trumpets to the light. I tend to find bindweed on the eastern and south-eastern sides of fields, where it climbs higher than on western and northern edges. That is, if I find it at all, for, like all 'weeds', field bindweed is suppressed with pesticides. Only when the field has not been sprayed too intensively does it have a chance of opening its pink trumpets to the sun. Its ability to defy destruction is what distinguishes this plant from others.

This resilience came to mind after the tsunami and nuclear reactor disaster in Fukushima in March 2011. I contacted a teacher from the city and offered to send her some morning glory seeds to plant. She and her pupils scattered the seeds in the place to which they had been evacuated. The children appreciated the chocolates, toothbrushes, balloons, and other small gifts sent to them, showing that even people in far-away Europe were concerned about their fate, but the letters they sent me said how much they also valued seeing the morning glory springing up: a sign of hope after so much devastation.

Japanese morning glory originally came from China, the seeds most likely arriving alongside medicinal herbs traded between the two nations. It thrived in Japan's volcanic soil, and the flowers came to be highly regarded: from 1804 to 1830, a competition to find the most beautiful morning glory was even held in Edo, as Tokyo was then known. Since then, two special markets have been taking place annually in Tokyo: the Asagao Ichi (morning glory market) in Iriya from 6 to 8 July, and the Hozuki

Ichi (Japanese lantern plant market) in Sensoji from 9 to 10 July. Many patterns, above all the stylised motifs on summer kimonos and fans, show the importance of these flowers as a seasonal symbol in Japan. Growing morning glory and watching it flower early in the day is my personal way of expressing my deep connection with my childhood and culture.

Setting aside the infrequent good summers, it's a miracle that these delicate plants manage to cope with the inclemency of Central European weather each year. Even if it has been battered by hailstones or pelted by rain, given a few sunny days, the morning glory will still direct its orchestra of trumpets towards the sun — even if the weather only allows it at the start of autumn.

In a different way, I also cherish the morning glory's counterpart from tropical America, which I grow on the patio: the passion flower. Its blooms are delicate works of art, much more ornate than the simple trumpets of the morning glory. With their almost bizarre, mysterious beauty, I cannot resist having one or two of them climbing and flowering on the patio each year. I have to seek out their flowers, which are often obscured by finger-shaped leaves. They also open in the morning, and close in the evening, albeit more slowly.

Named after the Passion of Christ, the uniqueness of the passion flower's structure must have so overwhelmed those who discovered the plant that, believing such beauty must have some higher meaning, they created a connection between the flower and the suffering of Jesus. For non-Christians, it is strange to imagine the crown of thorns and nails of the Crucifixion in this flower, and to equate it with, of all things, the death of a martyr.

An awful lot of plants have very strange names when you take them literally, owing to their various cultural origins. I cannot warm to the name of the passion flower, but I can enjoy its beauty. I watch wasps visiting its flowers, milling around as if attending a colourful annual funfair. With their yellow and black stripes, they match the flower's extravagance. Big bumblebees also board this floral merry-go-round, and wispy hoverflies lightly touch the petals. The taste of the passion fruit is as unique in the world of flavours as the flower's structure is in the visual world, but the plant only rarely forms fruits. If the flowers are not pollinated by the evening, when they close, then they have for ever missed their chance.

The morning glory and the passion flower have tropical origins, something that is not only seen in the shape of their blooms — my husband tells me there is no comparable flower from a temperate climate — but also in that they flower prolifically. They produce up to a dozen new buds daily for months, rather than mere days or weeks like the plants of our latitude. The red poppy blazes and glows with a new flower each day for maybe a week, and then its show is over. The season of the wild roses lasts from just a few days to a little over a week depending on the weather. Cultivated hybrid roses bloom out of sync, no longer bound to a region or its annual cycle. In contrast, the plants of tropical or sub-tropical origin can be admired consistently all summer, lending the garden a certain timelessness. I enjoy blooming roses, but morning glory and passion flower delight me.

I grow a buddleja and lantanas — the latter also being of tropical origin — on the patio for the moths and butterflies who visit the garden. The winged creatures that visit their flowers during the day are subtly elegant, for instance the hummingbird hawk-moth or the silver Y moth, which has a small silver Y on its forewings, only visible when closely observed. These migrant moths are both increasingly reliant on finding garden replacements for flowers that no longer grow here in the wild.

I also hope that the caterpillars of the oleander hawk-moth are munching on my oleander, or those in the town square or at the castle in nearby Burghausen. If the weather is favourable in May or June, these moths, bearing an impressive majestic green pattern, will be able to find host plants for their caterpillars north of the Alps, although oleander must be grown in pots, since our winters are too cold to plant it in the ground. As masses of summer tourists pass through Bavaria and the Alps on their way south to the regions in which oleander thrives, I think of the moths who have just made the same journey in reverse. Then, as the human summer holiday ends, the next generation of moths heads to warmer climes.

Like birds, the instincts of migratory butterflies don't allow for a summer holiday. Migration is a serious business. I am confronted with this fact in July and August, as the last swift of the season flies past, and the evening news reports huge traffic jams as holidaymakers head south. The conclusion I draw is that humans — and I include myself here — have migration in the blood.

This was dramatically brought to the fore when borders were closed due to COVID-19. For many, not being able to travel was almost a greater burden than the danger of infection. The limits and restrictions rankled with us. COVID-19 had spread as a result of humans travelling back and forth around the globe and, in turn, it was those fond of travelling who were perhaps hit hardest by the restrictions. Not even our gardens, which had never before been so intensively cared for, nor our gleaming basements, tidier than ever, could lessen our urge to see the world.

Musing about freedom and its limits only temporarily distracts me from the fruits ripening in my garden. Of course, holidays aren't the only way to relax; it can also be restorative to stay at home, watching, week by week, as the grapes on a vine turn purple, apples swell, and — despite many adversities — fine cabbage heads form and serpentine pumpkin tendrils take ownership of the vegetable patch.

I sometimes observe this growth with wonder, the aroma of raspberries filling my nose and mouth. The berries, which are only ripening now, are free of the wormy larvae of the raspberry beetle because they have developed outside of the insect's season. Herein lies another lesson from the garden about timing and processes, similar to the one learnt from falling apples; nearly all the ones that fall from the tree are 'wormy'. The caterpillars of the codling moth grow inside them, even if the apple is on the ground and the tree is no longer supplying the fallen fruit with nutrition.

The days in July and August can be hot and muggy; masses of warm air move in from the south-west and cause storms. In the late afternoon or evening, I like to sit in the corner shaded by the birch tree. The rustle of its leaves has a calming effect on me, even when I can barely feel a whisper of a breeze. Above me, titmice perform gymnastics on the branches, while in front of me, long-legged crane flies stalk over the grass — blackbirds and sparrows don't really like eating them, so they can flit about unharmed. I breathe in the scent of birch, combined with thuja and a hint of lavender blown over by a gentle gust from the gazebo: time to meditate.

I practise an outwardly directed meditation, as I call it. It is similar to the meditation I undertake during walks in woodland or by the river. I do not need to force myself to do it. Close enough to touch, a small black-and-gold-striped hoverfly hangs in the air, as if it is trying to work out whether I am a flower or some other useful thing. Its presence is enough for me to begin my meditation. Its wings flap so quickly that it gives me the impression that the small fly's body is encased in a pearly shimmer. I focus my eyes on it, and the many thoughts randomly shooting though my head disappear. For a fraction of a moment, the hoverfly becomes the centre of the world: it becomes Zen.

What more could I want?

Next to me, on the branches of the cherry laurel, a male blackbird plucks at the ripening berries. As if lost in thought, he sings a few verses, so quietly that I can barely hear them even though I am sitting no further than two metres away. I think that the male blackbird could also be meditating in his own way. Perhaps it is the end of breeding season, and he is free of the burden of raising a brood; he can just sit in the branches and enjoy the evening ambience. He briefly shakes his perfectly gleaming plumage, strokes his red-tipped yellow beak over his shoulder, and sings again for a second. Then he hops on to the lawn, head cocked to the side to listen, and begins his evening search for insects and worms. A few yellow leaves waft down from the birch.

Autumn

We cultivate stereotypes. They simplify not only the process of classification, but also maybe even thinking itself. My homeland of Japan is associated with two seasonal clichés: cherry blossom in spring and the red blaze of Japanese acers in autumn. By contrast, summer and winter don't really have specific colours associated with them, colours that would encapsulate the landscape and be described in haiku poetry. Looking at my garden, I frequently reflect on the impact of the changing colours over the days and months. Other than the most obvious tones, like the red of ripe tomatoes or the velvety purple of grapes, whose delicate, waxy sheen indicates that we can soon devour them, I cannot think of any 'typical' summer colours.

There is green, of course, in a multitude of shades. But what is green, exactly? Distinguishing it from blue assumes knowledge. The hues blend into each other, as the ocean changes colour as you move from the high seas towards land. In Japanese, we do not distinguish between blue and green as precisely as in European languages. Maybe it is because summer monsoon rain hits Japanese islands at exactly the same time that green vegetation is unfurling most vigorously. The dark clouds and floods dilute its intensity.

In autumn, the light returns as green bids its farewell, becoming yellow, pale ochre, brown, and, above all, red. Then, Japanese maple forests glow like a never-ending sunset, offering hope that the approaching typhoons will not be so bad. In Germany, the autumn generally brings a longer period of atmospheric calm. The sun has grown mild, even at midday, and the evenings are cool. Sometimes, both time and season appear to stand still; day follows day with no change in the weather.

In English, this autumn phase is called an Indian summer, but the German word for it is *Altweibersommer*, meaning 'old hags' summer'. It is a strange name, one that might drop out of use. Personally I find it quite charming — it refers to silver strands of hair, of which I have a few. In the 'old hags' summer', hair-like threads drift over the countryside on the autumn breeze. This lustrous, silvery silk is loaded with tiny cargo: spider babies. They embark on a flight into the unknown, attached to the strands, ending up wherever the wind's gusts see fit to take them. Occasionally, they land in my garden, but these small spiders and their thread parachutes have become a rarity. My husband tells me that in days gone by, the meadows in the floodplains would be so densely covered with the webbing that they shone in the morning light. But this spectacle was already consigned to the past when I arrived in Germany, removing silver from the muted colour spectrum of a German autumn.

Even red is barely present here. At best, it can be found in large parks. In my garden, only the acer takes on the unrivalled red that awakens my senses in the dwindling daylight. The autumnal colours of European trees span the range from yellow to dark brown. The yellows, with the exception of the bright yellow of birch leaves, appear somewhat dirty. These shades reveal too starkly that the leaves are perishing, making me appreciate the vivid-yellow birch leaves all the more. After floating down, they create a multi-faceted pattern on the now-sallow lawn.

As the weeks go by, children have fun picking out images in the patterns created by the randomly falling birch leaves. For some, this childish game continues into adulthood. They seek patterns in the clouds, attempt to interpret waves, or mark out constellations in the dark night sky, ascribing meanings to the images they pick out. For me, it's enough simply to admire the individual, lemon-yellow birch leaves and watch them fall, one by one, to the grass until a brown-tinged, golden carpet develops around the large tree.

Much more delicate in appearance is the scattering of palmate leaves from my Japanese acer. Set against the yellow of the birch, its blood red holds a captivating beauty that encourages meditation. It remains like that for a while — a week, even two. But then, if I want to enjoy whitlow-grass, speedwell, the blue cones of the common bugle next spring, or even the radial white suns of the daisies in the winter weeks when no snow is on the ground, I must clear the autumn leaves away. They are now waste to us — which is what they already were to the trees, becoming biocompost and humus, which is how it should be.

The changing colours signal the start of this process; the green has fulfilled its duties. Valuable nutrients have been stored in the birch, the acer, and all the shrubs in my hedge so that they can grow new leaves next year. What cannot be stored goes into the compost. We all know it. Yet, it somehow hurts, every autumn, to let go of this last flare of fading life.

Start of Winter

The rose is the queen of the garden. I discovered this just after arriving in Europe. Roses here are the flower-seller's staple, especially dark-red ones, but while they are also well liked in Japan, chrysanthemums — called *kiku* — are preferred. Perhaps it is because the *kiku* hasn't been in Europe long enough to earn admiration like the rose has here, having only arrived in 1789. Its botanical group name, winter aster, isn't commonly used — maybe because its Latin botanical name, chrysanthemum, meaning 'with golden flowers', is so well chosen.

Chrysanthemum sounds more elegant than rose, and the name is suitably exotic. Considered an expression of genteel modesty, it is originally from East Asia, where it was already a well-loved garden plant with many cultivars five centuries before Christ, in the time of Confucius. As an unpretentious symbol of the Japanese emperor (the *tennō*), the sixteen-petalled chrysanthemum became the national flower of Japan, with the *tennō* ruling the country from the symbolic Chrysanthemum Throne. As in the case of the grasses and blooms used in *ikebana* (Japanese flower-arranging), it is the chrysanthemum's simple beauty that gives it such power.

Around 1700, when Imperial Europeans were increasingly coming to East Asia, there were already 300 chrysanthemum cultivars, a similar number to that of rose varieties. Whereas, in the West, a rose with even the slightest variation in colour or petal shape was given its own name, often referencing a person, in Japan, this was not the case. From an East Asian perspective, the European culture of naming suggests an undue, seemingly boastful form of egocentrism — even if the flower variety was named after a wife or lover, rather than the rose-breeder themselves.

Admittedly, I had little knowledge of chrysanthemums when I came to Europe. It took me years to realise that they are a part of the daisy and aster family. On the other hand, roses in Europe were impossible to miss. They could be seen everywhere, adorning parks and gardens, ranging in size from fine discs similar to apple or cherry blossom to hand-sized specimens so drenched in colour that you would be forgiven for thinking that a heavy summer rain would smudge them. Some rose varieties have a glorious scent, while others charm with nuances of colour, masses of blooms, or such striking individual flowers that each one may be considered a work of art.

Larger but still delicate, rich-yellow chrysanthemum flower heads are mainly used as grave decorations in Germany. This is in contrast to Japan, where people wish each other a long life by gifting them to the living. I find it depressing when I see bunches of the yellow spheres on graves; they stand out against the black earth, as if artificially illuminated. The graves should look clean when the collective grave visits take place in Germany on All Saints' Day. In a strange way, it's touching that chrysanthemums from the Far East adorn graves here. The flower's Eastern connotations of long life must be a bitter irony for Westerners using them to mourn a loved one.

To me, moss and winter-flowering heather, which bears delicate pink bells during the bleakest season, seem like much more appropriate decorations to lay on a grave in memory of a loved one. This opinion is a result of my cultural background; I have found that emotions associated with specific plants are hard to change. I would even rather place a late rose on a grave as a sign of mourning, having seen how the late roses in the garden bloom even through snow and frost, bracing themselves against the withering cold.

In the garden, I labour in vain to protect my roses, as winter always wins the day in the end. However, with a persistence at which I reverently wonder, these flowers keep fighting well into the cold months. In December, just as the year is drawing to a close, they sometimes even wear a cap of snow. I find this one of the most touching images of the season. To me, the snow-topped rose has become a symbol both of resistance and of transience.

I watch with fascination as the night's snow starts to melt. The loose, sparkling bonnets of snow covering each rose grow soft and damp. Drop by drop, they melt, until the flower looks as if it has only been touched by the dew of a cool night. As the departing clouds reveal the sun, the rose bears witness to something even more miraculous: a visit from a tiny yellow-and-black-striped fly. These marmalade hoverflies float, seemingly weightless, towards the rose, rest on it, and then suddenly disappear again as if vanishing into thin air. Next to their fragility, the ice-crystal-encrusted rose looks almost chunky, its thorns clearly visible now that the lustrous leaves that conceal them in the summer are gone.

Since it is pointless to delay the inevitable, I must now overcome the plants' defences: the rosebushes in front of the living-room window are in need of their winter prune. Cut back to knee-high stumps, they will survive weeks, or even months, of frost. Frosts capable of bringing lows of minus twenty degrees Celsius were unknown to me when I lived in southern Japan, just as a rigorous prune of the shrub roses was. That this treatment makes my roses bloom even more beautifully the next summer is one of the biggest mysteries of the plant world to me. Despite the results, lopping off these stems pains me, and not only because the rose thorns sometimes pierce my skin.

Thorns are intended to protect roses from being nibbled by animals. Deer and, more frequently, goats graze on small trees and bushes in the mountainous regions of the Middle East — the homeland of the cultivated rose. The wild-growing dog roses of Europe are similarly defended, as are blackthorns — although the latter are armed with much more pointed and dangerous thorns. After I ready the rosebush for winter, my rigorous cuts with the secateurs come back to haunt me as I imagine every reason it might now have not to bloom next summer.

A new way of looking at the plant world has become popular in recent years. Some people are beginning to think that plants communicate, that they can even 'talk' to each other. It seems a bit over the top to me, but of course, trees and bushes do react to injuries. If their tissues are cut or damaged, they need to produce chemicals both to seal the wound and to prevent a bacterial infection. As I understand it, insects respond to the release of such protective chemicals in the same way that they do to the colours, forms, and scents of flowers.

Nature's interactions are fascinating, but interpreting these phenomena as a kind of speech humanises plants too much. Does the grass in a meadow also call out for cows to come and graze on it, because otherwise it would become overgrown and turn into a forest? Such philosophies confuse me much more than they help me to understand the processes of nature.

While contemplating my rosebushes late in December, I notice the groups of primulas that are flowering close to them. Since October, their pale-yellow petals with golden centres have been catching my eye, even though I haven't been paying special attention to them. I gave just as little heed to the daisies, which are now experiencing their second bloom of the year on the moss-covered lawn. Both will flower the whole way through winter's snows and into spring.

Between the thorny stems of the rosebushes, the fleshy green leaves of primulas form rosettes. Their flowers are barely elevated from the leaves, which is why the snow doesn't squash them. I have never been able to determine why they are so hardy, when it doesn't even snow in their Atlantic homelands. It is just another mystery thrown up by life in the garden.

The late period in the garden always provokes such thoughts. Little, almost nothing, changes in the weeks from dull November to frosty January. Even so, in some years, winter keeps us waiting. The garden illustrates how artificial such categories are. The seasons have no fixed boundaries; they will come and go in their own time, whatever the calendar says.

Winter Solstice

My barefoot morning walks in the garden continue into the colder months, even if the excursion comprises just a few steps. The late-autumn cool is invigorating; I like the tingling stimulation I get from the frost-covered grass in the morning, radiating upwards from the soles of my feet. When the temperature is hovering around zero, and the pressure from my feet melts the frost, the rimy grass reveals my footprints, as tiny icicles drift down from the birch. On such early-winter mornings, time stands still.

The nights sleep on into the morning, and the evenings come fast, yet still subtly enough that I don't notice the light change. When snow falls, the light reflecting off it lifts my mood.

Each year, I grow more impatient for the arrival of the winter solstice, and the lengthening of the days that follows. Despite experience to the contrary, I always believe things will pick up afterwards. Ironically, the weather is frequently particularly foul on this eagerly anticipated day. I console myself by remembering that the rain does the garden good; it revives life in the soil, setting it in motion again if an early frost has forced it into dormancy. Many more frosts will come after the solstice, and even these are 'good'. I admit that my own feelings about the weather are not in harmony with what is necessary for the plants. I can't avoid my negative emotions, but I can establish a little distance from them.

One of the season's challenges is that I have little insight into what is really happening in the garden; in inclement weather I cannot lie on the wintery earth with a magnifying glass in my hand to inspect the small details, nor can I listen as the blackbird does, with his head so endearingly held to the side. I have to assume a lot, or learn from books or from what I have been told. However, on afternoons when the low sun casts rays of light, I can sometimes still see life: a life that moves in the downward and upward vacillations of a set of tiny shimmering wings.

I draw pleasure from watching the dance of the winter crane flies. Here and there, wherever the sun happens to shine and provide heat for their flight, they twirl in loose swarms, as if in slow motion. Ten or so male flies, sometimes even up to three dozen of them, perform acrobatics to attract females. The air temperature is only a few degrees above freezing, but the sun's rays have enough warmth to them to prompt this dance. Despite patches of snow still lying on the ground, the winter crane flies draw energy from the sun's warmth to shoot almost vertically upwards, reaching a height of up to two metres, then glide a little lower in order to zip straight back up again. Against the light, their bodies form a silver column.

At the moment, there are no birds that want to catch these crane flies. It means that they can dance and dance until the shadows come, when they disappear. Should a night frost occur, they can survive it. Having started dancing in autumn, the all-male dance troop will eventually be visited by some females, come to mate. Even more than the freshly blossoming hellebores, it is the arrival of these fragile creatures that gives me the feeling that spring is here. I am moved, every time I see them.

Above, in the branches of the birch, blue tits chatter, taking no notice of the crane flies. Sparrows perform effortful and rather inelegant gymnastics to reach the fat balls I hang from the tree. A few chaffinches with their old-rose breast plumage are searching the grass for flakes of fat that the sparrows have managed to dislodge from the balls. A sparrowhawk speeds by overhead, his appearance sending the sparrows racing into the bushes at breakneck speed. The garden is now full of life; all it needed was a couple of minutes of sun. Right now, I can clearly sense why Amaterasu, the sun goddess of Ancient Japan, is seen as being at the root of everything, and understand the profound symbolic meaning behind the rising sun on our flag — a sun that ascends over Japan each morning from out of the deep expanse of the Pacific Ocean.

Until recently, people were entirely dependent on the light and power of the sun for energy, and its place in folk culture was accordingly central. I discovered that in Europe, a long time ago, Yuletide was celebrated at the start of the sun's return to the dark northern latitudes. Christianity appropriated this pagan festival, reinventing it as Christmas, but its association with the sun remained, deeply rooted in our senses.

A new annual cycle begins with the winter solstice, but the deepest cold is still to come, as late as March. Trees, animals, roots, and soil life are in a state of suspension: this period requires patience. My ability to wait gives me a sense of how far I have come with my Zen Buddhist mindset. If 'the journey is the destination', then even waiting for the journey to begin must be part of my objective. It pervades my work in the garden, for I must wait patiently: not only to be able to harvest something that I have worked hard to grow, but also to be ready for the unexpected, which is the spice of gardening, and can spark so much joy. On the threshold of a new year, I look forward to the bliss of gardening, embracing it as it comes and trying to make the best of it.

Among the undergrowth of thin branches in a corner of the garden, a wren creeps, like a mouse. It pauses for a moment before belting out a song into the winter evening. I take it as evidence of a good start to the new year.

II.

Aspects of Garden Life

Rose Chafers and Harlequin Ladybirds

A flash of bright green darts through the garden. In front of the roses, it slows and becomes more visible, glowing like an emerald in the light before throwing itself into the bushes, causing them to shake and swing about. With up to half its body plunged into a flower, the green beetle drills past a rose's inner petals into the loose cushion of the stamen. Its protruding rear resembles a piece of polished bronze reflecting fragments of light.

Any attempt gently to touch its body results in it slipping through my fingers and sliding further into the flower. On a second try, its hind legs, equipped with thorn-like defences, fend me off. I'm under no illusion that it wants to be caught: several times, a rose chafer has demonstrated how quickly and elegantly it can fly out of my hand. It happens so suddenly that I normally do not register the moment of take-off. The smoky-brown membranes of its hindwings protrude from small slits on the side of its body and immediately begin to buzz. After a lightning-fast launch, its metallic green flashes as it flies. To take off, it doesn't even need first to raise its brittle elytra — hardened, case-like forewings — as May and June bugs, regulars of this garden, do. Without air resistance pressing against rigid elytra sheaths, its flight is faster and nimbler. Its body is completely smooth, as if polished, perfectly designed for flight, and magnificent in its lustre. It is a beetle that bathes in the light of the south.

I remember seeing similar beetles in the flower-laden hedges and gardens of my childhood in Japan's subtropical south. Back then, I could only recognise the ladybirds; children's eyes are used to seeing things without necessarily understanding what they are. Children register their fast movement and shine, followed by their sudden disappearance, without ascribing any meaning to these fleeting impressions.

I had forgotten about the red-and-black beetles of the early summers of my childhood until I saw something similar in Europe. It was a different species, of course, but one so similar it was as if it had followed me. Ladybirds are very common in almost all of Europe, and my garden is home to some. Their appearance is unmistakable: small domes with colourful spots and tiny legs that can run away with surprising speed. Or they suddenly fly off, lifting their elytra, as most common beetles must, to allow them to take off.

I hope they are heading in the direction of the aphids with which I constantly do battle. Yet, I already know that in the fight against the aphids, ladybirds do less than they should. These beetles are Asian ladybirds, East Asian to be precise. They are beetles that live in my homeland and that I may have already seen as a child but failed to notice. They were imported into greenhouses in Europe in order to keep down aphid numbers. Locked in, they performed their assigned task quite well. Naturally, some of them got out. They survived and bred in the freedom of their new world, where there were already numerous other species of ladybird. The native species did not eat aphids as diligently nor multiply as quickly as the new arrivals from the East.

These non-native beetles have been named harlequin ladybirds in Europe because they are so varied in colour and pattern. They can look the same as almost all European ladybird species, which causes confusion, even among creepy-crawly connoisseurs. Now, a two-spot ladybird is no longer always a two-spot ladybird, nor is a seven-spot ladybird always a seven-spot ladybird; harlequin ladybirds can masquerade as both.

I heard about this 'problem' when I started trying to make the ladybirds' existence in my garden as comfortable as possible. They were to be my allies in the battle against aphids. From that perspective, it would seem that a lot of ladybirds could only be a good thing. However, I was told that a lot of ladybirds is actually a problem. For a decade now, the most commonly seen bugs have been harlequin ladybirds. The argument goes that they don't belong here and ought to be returned to greenhouses because they are destroying our native beetle species. Although this argument sounds convincing, it does not persuade me. How could the two-spot or seven-spot ladybirds be pushed out, when all species of ladybird working together don't even get close to eradicating aphids?

There are always enough of these insects left over for the native ladybirds in my garden, confirmed by repeated sightings of vast aphid buffets every May and June, which force me temporarily to disable my Buddhist stance towards other living creatures. I attempt to destroy these pests using any biological means I can, such as nettle manure or soapberry spray. I draw the line at man-made chemical poisons, however.

I find myself thinking of ladybirds while admiring the rose chafers. Aphids also cling to the roses, and I spot a small harlequin ladybird crawling over to them. It doesn't seem to notice the large rose chafer. Paying it attention would be unnecessary; it poses no threat to the ladybird. Barely any creatures harm the harlequin ladybird or its European relatives; they are protected by their awful-tasting blood, which they excrete from their knees and allow to run down their legs. Given their prevalence and survival skills, one would think there would be enough ladybirds around for me to stop my aphid destruction and calmly admire their natural pest control.

The rose chafer's larvae have an unappetising appearance. They are fat, creamy, blue-red shimmering grubs that live in the compost. When I put my hands in the compost to test its readiness, I dig them up, sometimes in great numbers. If I didn't know that they would become magnificent rose chafers, I would probably lay them out as appetisers for the blackbirds, as I do with the similar but considerably smaller June bug larvae. I do this because, in some spots in the garden, June bug larvae eat way too much of the grass, creating bald patches that look as if they have been scorched.

In the extremely dry April of 2020, I found a rose chafer in the compost that, at first glance, appeared dead. However, it was not — after I laid it on the windowsill, it flew off. It had looked so dead when I first saw it; its legs did not even stick out from its body, instead they were pressed against its abdomen. I could roll it like a long elliptical ball. The bug had emerged from its chrysalis the previous autumn and had spent the winter in a small cavity in the compost. Had I not dug it up in April, it would have crawled out by itself, in May at the latest, and flown away to look for a partner.

Maybe it's the same beetle that is now bathing in the scent of the roses while eating pollen to give it strength for the coming days. My compost was not in the least depleted by it and the numerous other rose chafers that lived in it as grubs. I ponder this as I watch its emerald-green lustre on the delicate yellow of the rose. These beetles fly so quickly that birds can barely catch them, and even if they do, the rose chafers are too hard to be swallowed and too slippery to break open. They are not food for the woodpeckers in the garden, or even the faster and more nimble blackbirds.

Years ago, in Istria, we once saw a large, yellow-legged gull throwing a rose chafer, which it had somehow caught, on to the stony ground, like the crows at home do with walnuts. It picked at the beetle's exploded body. Was it worth it? Flying costs seagulls energy. Maybe these birds find it fun to treat beetles like that. However, this is unusual, and the rose chafer population is certainly not at risk from this strange gull behaviour.

They fit together: the rose chafers and harlequin ladybirds. They are both beautiful in their own special way, their lifestyles are interesting, and I find them in my garden year after year. I take note of harlequin ladybirds when I see them. Sometimes, I place them directly in a colony of aphids so that they can fulfil their destiny, even if they have never been prevalent enough that I could give up my struggle against the aphids. I take delight in every rose chafer: they are beautiful and have never eaten all my compost, which was my original concern. My wishful thinking did not come to pass, nor did my fear come true. The essential nature of the garden remains a mystery to me. And that is why I admire it, every day, year in, year out.

Fireflies and Other Beetles

My garden has more beetles to offer than just shiny rose chafers and spherical, spotted ladybirds. I find fireflies the most captivating of all my garden's insects. When they dance aglow around the garden in the late midsummer twilight, my thoughts disappear, and I slip into a feeling of deep peace. My eyes follow the loops and arches they draw in the air, cutting through the deep shadows of the bushes in the already advancing dusk, leaving traces of light for a child's hand to catch.

Fireflies awaken memories of days now distant, both in time and in geography. I see children walking with lanterns on an early-summer evening in Japan, the soft light of trapped fireflies shining from them. People used to do this in Europe, too, long ago. It was said that you could read by the light of the fireflies, which could be true for the large letters of the Latin alphabet, but I cannot imagine you would be able to read Japanese symbols; the dots and dashes that give them meaning are so tiny.

The children carrying fireflies in lanterns on warm summer nights certainly did not want to read; they wanted to enjoy the atmosphere created by the insects' luminescence. One image that comes to mind is of a boy accompanying a girl as they walk along a dark path, holding a small cage of fireflies. I freely admit that seeing the glimmering insects makes me feel romantic. Who can escape their magic?

Since becoming aware that the firefly larvae eat snails, I have loved these little summer lights even more. I am a little embarrassed by this bias; I know that just as I welcome the traces of light drawn by fireflies, I should also accept the snails in my garden. The many snails. The more the better for the fireflies. I wonder why they don't eat slugs, too. Are they too slimy? Maybe the firefly larvae just haven't tried the rich buffet of slugs. I think about this as I watch the fireflies' dance.

On such evenings, I can often observe the movements of another beetle. They begin to wake just after the sun has set, but while it's still light and the beetles are easily visible. Buzzing, they come out of the garden, looking as though they are about to take a tour of the house. They do flying loops on the patio, ascend to balcony height, peer through the windows of the upper floor, and finally hurry away over the roof. After a couple of turns in the sky, they return to seek out birch leaves. I don't know if they eat them; at this point they are too high to see, and it is almost dark, almost time for the fireflies.

These creatures are June bugs, which visit my garden every year. The majority of them were once fat larvae living off the roots of the grass in the lawn. I find them under the stepping stones when cleaning the edges. If there isn't a large crowd of them, their root nibbling doesn't cause any damage. The beetles are a yellow brown, with fur-like hair on their underbellies, and are a bit like a smaller, paler version of the May bug. When I catch one, it scratches at my hand, but it does not try to bite me, as many other beetles do.

A large swarm of June bugs will not go unnoticed by the sparrows, who try to catch them while they are still crawling on the grass, before the beetles become airborne and nimble. The sparrows' failed attempts make me laugh. They are simply not flycatchers, yet they still give it a try. They clearly like the taste of the June bugs, but they only eat ever the abdomens, leaving the legs, wings, and heads behind.

There are also May bugs in the garden. The true common May bug is also known as the cockchafer and is not to be confused with the forest cockchafer, which lives in light deciduous forests. As their name suggests, they are active from the end of April to mid-May, about two months earlier than June bugs. A relative of the scarab beetle, they have distinctive fan-like antennae. Since I have been looking for them, I have noted that nearly all the May bugs found in my garden are male. They come from far away, in search of females. We generally only ever spot a couple of specimens. The days when, every three years, massive clouds of May bugs would swarm, stripping the trees, are long gone; I have only heard about them.

In the forest alongside the River Inn, we come across the May bug more frequently, though its appearance is still rather erratic from one year to the next. There is not even a hint of the mass swarms that used to come every three years — the time it takes for a May bug grub to develop. We were all the more surprised a couple of years ago when, on a walk in an alluvial forest, we found some marten dung full of May bug remains. The fowl that were once fed these large beetles, or the falcons that cleverly snatch them from the air, are not the only ones who find May bugs delicious.

A more unusual garden visitor is the long, thin, green or bluey-violet musk beetle. Its body is two to two and a half centimetres long, with feelers of a similar length, which are bow-shaped, and remain so even in flight. When a musk beetle flies past, it looks like a very small model aircraft. Its flight is dead straight, but the skewed posture it adopts while flying is unusual, its long feelers adding drama. Its musky smell most likely serves to protect it against birds or large bats, which would otherwise have an easy time plucking this beetle out of the summer evening air as it flies.

I have a very special relationship with the musk beetle, stemming from the time that one landed on me in such a way that I could look it directly in the face. I was amazed, but it seemed unimpressed by me. Since I was in the process of eating watermelon, I offered it a piece. It ate the fruit from my fingers, dribbling juice. After that, it did not want to let me go. It clung to my finger and sucked on the remains of the melon, its strong jaws making a chewing motion as it drank the sticky juice drop by drop. Since then, I have been on close terms with musk beetles, and I love it when one occasionally flies through the garden. If circumstances allow, I catch the visitor and offer it an attractive piece of fruit. Melon remains a favourite.

Like most gardens, mine houses other, less flamboyant beetles, too. Learning their names and identifying them is a task for specialists. Two of these beetles arouse my interest, but in different ways. The first one, the hazelnut weevil, is so ugly, with its super long and thin proboscis, that when I first saw it, I could barely believe that such a creature could even exist. It has two feelers that protrude from its snout, adding to its particularly bizarre appearance. Generally, when animals have these kinds of special characteristics, they are used by males to impress females. But it is actually female hazelnut weevils that have the longest snouts, which they use to drill into ripening hazelnuts in order to lay their eggs in them. The larvae eat the inside of the nuts, which fall to the ground empty, allowing the larvae to crawl out and pupate. In spring, the beetles emerge just as new hazelnuts are forming.

Hazelnut weevils help themselves to a large proportion of my hazelnuts. However, the number of empty nuts in the forest is much larger than in my garden. Despite the effect they have on my crop, ultimately I can appreciate these beetles, with their grotesque Pinocchio noses, because they illustrate the inventive modifications nature is capable of producing on encountering something as enticing as hazelnuts. I really enjoy eating them, too.

Click beetles offer a different kind of surprise. They look as though their thoraxes and abdomens have been linked together with hinges, a trait that clearly distinguishes them from the average beetle. They get their name from the miniature circus trick they can perform. When placed on its back, a click beetle can propel itself into the air and turn over with an audible click. Less amusing than their special way of righting themselves is the lifestyle of their larvae. They are called wireworms because they are as tough and supple as thick wire. Furthermore, they can give an unpleasant nip; I will have nothing to do with them, as even though they don't actively eat the roots of the lettuce or other plants, they certainly damage them. In the garden, there are several types of click beetle, differing in terms of size and colour. Clearly, as a family they are very successful, since there are many different species of them.

My relationship with beetles is like my relationship with butterflies. The more I learn about them, the more I realise just how many different species live in my small garden, and how they are impacted by what I do there. But I must also accept that some species exert an influence of their own. The garden is alive in its own right; it is not just an expression of my desires. Zen Buddhism always reminds me of this fact. Until 'enlightenment' comes to me, I will continue to see things from a practical perspective, too — which simply means entering into a set of reasonable compromises with the other creatures in my garden, including beetles.

Conversations with Blackbirds

I called the magnificent male blackbird Maxi. His plumage shimmered, velvety black, and a lustrous aura formed around him in the bright sunlight. He sported a golden-yellow beak with a reddish tip, and a fine, yet vibrant, yellowy-orange ring circled his eyes. A male blackbird would struggle to be any more majestic, and I was convinced that far and wide there was none more beautiful, or that could sing as stirringly and with as much variety as he could.

My admiration sprang from the fact that I was getting to see Maxi's splendour up close and personal; he regularly appeared as I started doing jobs in the garden. At first, he scanned the earth that I had freshly turned, while keeping a distance of two or three metres, but it wasn't long before he came a bit closer. He even started appearing as I was hanging out the washing to dry. When I carried the laundry basket out of the house, he would hop a few steps ahead of me to the exact spot where I usually started pegging out the washing. When I was finished, he would fly up to the birch and start singing, just a few metres away on one of the lower branches. As he warbled, I could see his brightly burnished beak, and his voice really did sound golden to me.

Of course, I convinced myself that he was singing for me. His song was particularly beautiful, and I occasionally told him so, as he hopped around me in the beds. In response he would cock his head to the side and look at me with one eye. With the other, he kept a watch on his surroundings. This was doubtless a necessary precaution, for before we had a dog, cats would regularly prowl through the garden, on the lookout for birds, as their nature dictates. When I went into the house, Maxi would sing a little louder.

I sometimes wondered whether he was fully fit. After all, it was spring. Should he not have already found a mate, and soon have chicks in his nest? I would push this question to the back of my mind when Maxi appeared and hopped around me. I never fed him. It never occurred to me to dig up worms for Maxi: he simply didn't look hungry to me. The notion that such a pretty bird felt comfortable being so close by was flattering.

In March, a large number of crocuses flowered in the garden. Some of them poked through the ground as yolk-yellow buds and opened their slim calyxes in the sunny weather. Others were of a similar size but bloomed in lilac or dark violet, while some of the smaller ones had light-blue petals. Strangely, the yellow crocuses began to perish almost as soon as they emerged. One after the other, they fell to the ground. The other colours remained standing and continued to flower gloriously for a week or longer in the cool days and lightly frosted nights.

With some concern, I reported the mysterious deaths of the yellow crocuses to my husband. He looked at me and said just one word, 'Maxi.' Responding to my rather baffled face, he explained, 'The yellow of the crocus is the exact same colour as the yellow on a male blackbird's beak. It functions as a trigger to attack. Maxi will be pecking and snapping at the crocuses. He's treating the flowers like an intruding male blackbird that has invaded his territory.'

'But the crocuses are not a blackbird,' I countered and added, 'Maxi wouldn't be so stupid!'

'Oh,' my husband answered, 'we should be under no such illusion. Robins have long been known to attack a tuft of reddish-brown feathers as if it were an actual robin.

They're reflex actions, pure and simple. Colour is a very effective trigger for aggressive behaviour. And Maxi doesn't have a female. So right now, he may well react particularly aggressively to anything that even vaguely resembles the yellow beak of another male blackbird.'

I found this explanation sobering because it forced me to consider how Maxi may have seen me. Maybe he did not regard me as a good fairy with whom he had been keeping company when I was in the garden. I suddenly stumbled upon the philosophical question 'What am I?' Who was I to this male blackbird? If I knew that, then I would know more than the great philosophers. Later, the question often came to mind when I was with my dog and looked him right in the eye. The looks we exchanged told me that we humans have no idea what is really happening in the heads of dogs and birds. Other creatures are full of the mysteries of life. As are we — after all, are we not merely flattering ourselves when imagining we truly understand our own nature?

The small blackbird challenged me to think about myself, more than my dog did. I was much closer to my pet than the bird. I got him as a very small puppy and nursed him myself. It meant he was very attached to me; he adored me as I did him. However, Maxi was an adult male blackbird who had come to me of his own volition. I had not tried to attract him; we simply met in the garden. In his avian way, he considered the garden his own territory, one that he defended. What could have moved him to want to be near me? He did not flirt with me, like a bird that had been reared and shaped by humans might do. Clearly, Maxi simply felt comfortable close to me.

Are there connections that we cannot see because we do not have a sense for them, invisible links with other creatures? I wanted to contemplate this question but could not find a way to begin. Deep in thought, I removed the limp yellow crocus flowers. Bees that visited the yellow flowers at this early stage in the year would miss them. However, I hoped Maxi would feel better without these silent rivals.

I would listen to him absentmindedly as he sang in front of the house in the evenings. Long and loudly, he warbled from the birch. His song sounded more intense in the early mornings than later in the day. He could almost be relied on as an alarm clock that would wake me up in time to take my dog for a walk. In the evenings, he would suddenly stop singing with the advancing dusk and start a shrill and fierce 'chink'. Straight away, the whole area would erupt into a chorus of 'chinks' in reply, the garden descending into acoustic hysteria. And then, almost as abruptly, silence would fall. The blackbirds had flown to their roosts, a bush safe from humans and cats, where they would spend the night.

Every evening, throughout the winter, they would return to their common roost, until the females came back from their winter migration to the Mediterranean, when they would pair off and claim fixed territories. The majority of male blackbirds stay in Germany. A few females do, too, but the vast majority fly south in the autumn and only return in the spring.

A few days after the execution of the yellow crocuses, Maxi actually found a mate. She acted much more timidly towards me than he did, but she accepted that he would continue to approach me in almost the same way as before. They built a concealed nest in our thuja hedge, and I often heard her call an alarm when a straying neighbourhood tomcat wandered through the garden. Maxi would attack it by diving at it repeatedly, which made the tomcat visibly uncomfortable, but did not bring the feline expeditions to an end.

I didn't get to see whether Maxi's brood was successful or not. He hardly had any time for me after the chicks had hatched and needed to be fed. However, I didn't fail to notice that his mate fed the brood much more than he did, and that Maxi sometimes flew rather far away into neighbouring gardens and sang there, even though his chicks, still in our hedge, had not yet fledged.

In the early summer, he stopped appearing. I missed him. The other male blackbird, who had already replaced him after a few days, was as much a stranger to me as I was to him. His song was different to Maxi's, and he never tried to come close to me. He was simply a blackbird, of which there are hundreds and thousands in gardens and parks. In contrast, Maxi had earned the right to a name, which made him into an individual. He had a personality that I found unique. Perhaps he became the victim of a cat or sparrowhawk? Or he got sick. Small birds die quickly and unnoticeably. I grieved for him.

The next spring, when the yellow crocuses flowered, and this time remained undamaged, I was reminded of him. Thoughtfully, I watched the bees as they crawled into the crocuses' deep golden petals. A blackbird once again trilled from the birch, but its song was unfamiliar. In the birdbox, which we had hung on the trunk of the tree, a couple of great tits were building their nest. They eagerly flew in, carrying moss and small feathers that had been dropped by pigeons promenading in the garden. The blackbirds were digging soil out of the pots in which I had planted lettuces, and proceeded to scatter it around. Naturally, very naturally, the life of the blackbirds in the garden continued.

Then, several generations of blackbirds later, a female blackbird flummoxed me. Just like every other year, we had a nesting pair of blackbirds in our garden. Or, looking at it from their point of view, the garden was part of this couple's territory. Both of them behaved unremarkably, neither shy nor overly curious, in the way that blackbirds do when they are familiar with humans and have integrated themselves into our world. The pair had already been in the garden for several weeks when we noticed that a second female had joined them, and that she was acting very strangely. She followed the first female around constantly, tailing her everywhere she went in search of food. If the first female flew away and over into the neighbours' gardens, the second female would follow. She would stay at a distance of at least half a metre, but the male, who was usually close by, sometimes attacked her. I thought he did it half-heartedly; he was never fierce enough to drive her away. Rather, he appeared to be baffled. Some days, we thought that the new female was trying to push out the first female, in order to win the male and his territory. But we never witnessed any attacks. The second female simply followed the first one around, as if pulled by an invisible string.

As the nest had been built in the hedge of the neighbour's garden, we did not see if the second female had contributed to its construction. However, when she repeatedly flew out of the garden with food in her beak, following the first female, we assumed that she was helping to feed the chicks. Could it be that the male had mated with two females and was raising a brood with them together? It can happen when there is a shortage of males. But it was unclear whether the second female had also laid eggs in the (joint?) nest or if she was just acting as a helper.

All that was unusual enough, but it got even stranger. Increasingly, the second female stayed in our garden on her own. By now it was May, and the young blackbirds nesting in the gardens should have fledged or been about to fledge. Was female number two no longer needed? Surprisingly, she began to behave in a similar fashion to Maxi. If I came into the garden, she didn't avoid me, and sometimes followed me. Soon, it seemed as though she was actually waiting for me under the star magnolia on the edge of the patio, or maybe she just felt comfortable there. Her behaviour became increasingly baffling. Eventually, she tolerated me being just an arm's length from her.

If I talked to Emma, as I was now calling her, she looked at me with her dark eyes. They were full of trust, I thought. Yet, something was different to how it had been with Maxi. I searched my memory, image by image, before realising the difference: Emma ruffled her feathers too much. She looked too big, too puffed up. She was sick, deadly sick, and getting weaker.

First thing every morning, I checked on her, and placed a crumbled hard-boiled egg close by in order to help build up her strength. With increasing frequency she hopped over to the birdbath to take a drink. Slowly, she would dip her inconspicuous brown beak, lift her head, and let the water run into her gullet. Again and again; too often for a healthy bird. One day, I thought that Emma was doing better, and that was the last time I ever saw her.

She had touched me deeply, but in a different way to Maxi. He had been healthy, in top form; I had no idea why he sought out my company and visibly enjoyed being close. With Emma, it was different; she only got to know me because I spent a lot of time in the garden. What was extraordinary was that it was only when she got sick that she sought proximity to a human. Several times, I noticed that after I had talked to her for a while, she would close her eyes and go to sleep as I worked in the beds next to her. Maxi would have been able to fly away at lightning speed should I have done anything that appeared dangerous to him, but Emma submitted herself to my protection. Why was this blackbird so trusting?

These two birds showed me that the deep divide between animals and humans, ingrained in Western philosophy, does not really exist. Emotional closeness is accepted with dogs and a few other pets, but it is mainly kept behind closed doors. I don't understand this divide. In my understanding, which has been shaped by Zen Buddhism, this schism does not exist. The more I work in the garden, the more clearly I recognise this.

Mowing the Lawn

When spring follows its normal course and gives us authentic, changeable April weather, a problem arises, one that I think about more intensely from year to year. The moss that, in the winter, gave the lawn its softness and yellowy-green colouring makes way for the growing grass. Sometimes, by the end of April, the blades are so long that I think it already needs to be mowed. If the spring is dry, it takes until May to reach this point. By then it has inevitably started; the juddering of lawnmowers can be heard throughout the whole neighbourhood. I feel the pressure to get down to the job, too, for a lawn must be cared for; otherwise, it would end up a wilderness. My neighbours do not like wild lawns. The verges, embankments, and green spaces in my town are tidily tended.

Although I know that it is high time to cut the lawn, I find myself debating an ever-deeper conflict. My many years of gardening have opened my eyes to the fact that mowing the grass can be very destructive. Its improving effect is only superficial: mowing has serious consequences. The more attention I pay to life in the garden, the clearer these consequences become.

One of the first casualties that gave me cause to ponder was an enchanting butterfly called the orange tip. They are seen on the wing in April or May, and I am especially happy to spot one in the garden. Only the males of this tiny white species have the orange tips on their wings that make them so recognisable from afar. The females, without any eye-catching colouring, resemble small cabbage whites and are consequently, far less noticeable. If they land on a cuckooflower, they can be observed close up. Then, the difference to the cabbage whites becomes visible: the underside of their hindwings is the same as that of the males', covered in beautiful moss-green marbling.

Orange-tip butterflies are beautiful and delicate. They are also perfectly harmless, since their caterpillars live on cuckooflowers and garlic mustard, which predominantly grow along forest paths and roads, meaning they don't cause any damage to gardens. We can simply admire the elegance of these spring butterflies. However, mowing is extremely harmful to these pretty insects, as it kills their caterpillars, wiping out the next generation.

Cuckooflowers don't grow in every garden. They require wet, preferably somewhat boggy soil, and in order to grow them, allowances must be made. I am happy to leave a couple of square metres of unmown grass with cuckooflowers among it for the orange-tip butterflies. But other cases are more complicated: the blue lycaenidae, also known as the blues, are one of the most striking butterflies and are now particularly rare. The wings of the males mirror the blue of the sky in a varied spectrum of tones; they are so beautiful that one species is even called the Adonis blue. In the garden, their worst enemies are lawnmowers, and in open spaces, maintenance measures, which cut down the caterpillars' host plants as well as damaging the nests of ants that build their colonies in grassed areas — caterpillars of some lycaenidae live in these nests. Other butterflies, which are not quite so distinguished in terms of their visible beauty, also need grasses for their caterpillars to feed on.

Lawnmowers are particularly devastating for all these creatures, as they can no longer live on the agricultural grasslands that were once meadows. These fields are cut four to five times a year, and all the cuttings are put into a silo or made into huge bales to be fed to cattle. Gardens provide one of the last suitable habitats for butterflies that can no longer live in the meadows. The same goes for wild bees and numerous other insects. Their disappearance is lamented, and the agriculture industry is being called upon to make land use more environmentally friendly. Yet, what do we do in our gardens and urban green spaces? Incessant destruction.

This kind of thinking besieges me when it is once again time to mow the lawn, and I begin worrying about the results. For example, previously I did not anticipate that frequent mowing creates food for slugs, since they particularly like the taste of the finely chopped grasses and herbs that are left lying around after every pass of the mower. Could a feasible way of keeping slugs away from my vegetable patch be to provide them with some grass cuttings as a distraction?

This experiment ended in immediate disappointment. Even slugs go for quality; they preferred my juicy lettuce, kohlrabi, and other vegetables to the chopped grass. Large slugs can afford to be choosy, while only the smaller ones, which I notice less, really benefit from what the mower leaves behind. The big ones made their way purposefully towards the lettuce as usual, as I saw from the slime trails they left behind when I went into the garden in the morning. It is even easier for them to move over the mowed lawn than through tall grass.

All this puts me off mowing the lawn even more. However, it's not that simple, because of worms. I see these creatures when I am turning the beds. Where the soil is good and light, I find large and clearly well-nourished worms. Apparently, an awful lot of them live under golfing greens, provided these haven't been treated with poisons to kill weeds. The reason is clear: mowing provides worms with finely chopped vegetation to eat.

This is not only good for worms, but also for the larvae of the various insects that live on plant parts which gradually decay on the surface of the soil, for instance the larvae of large, long-legged crane flies. Despite their somewhat threatening appearance and the myth that they bite, crane flies are completely harmless. Crane fly larvae do also eat roots, so when there are large numbers of them, they can damage plants. That doesn't happen in my garden, though, maybe because enough of them are enthusiastically hunted and devoured by blackbirds and starlings, who do their best scavenging after the lawn has been mown. Our blackbirds and the neighbourhood starlings appear and immediately start a rigorous search of the freshly mown areas. When the grass is too long, I get a creeping feeling that the blackbirds are looking at me, asking when we will finally mow the lawn so they can easily hop around on the earth. The long grass impedes them. Robins also need areas of short grass, and hedgehogs do, too. It allows them to search for worms and snails without impediment.

Taking hedgehogs, blackbirds, starlings, robins, worms, and soil-dwelling insects into consideration, I should mow the lawn. Yet, further findings and discoveries in the garden reveal even more problems. Before turning into the interesting swarms of beetles that took flight in the evenings around the summer solstice, the fat larvae of the June bugs and their larger relatives, the May bugs, ate so many grass roots that brown patches appeared, dotted around the lawn. If hedgehogs are doing well in the garden, then robins are having a hard time: robins build their nests in shrubs on the ground, but then hedgehogs come along and eat the eggs or chicks. Even hedgehogs and robins cannot give me clarity in weighing up the pros and cons of mowing. My own emotions are added to the mix. I don't want to leave the garden to its own devices and watch it become a wilderness, so I have no choice other than to accept that while mowing may damage some plants and animals, it benefits others. It means that I more thoroughly assess when and how I will mow; its frequency is not exactly rationally scheduled, but rather based on my gut feeling.

The timing depends very much on the development of certain plants. I would like the common bugle with its beautiful blue flowers to have enough time to spread its seeds. At the end of April and the start of May, when the bugle is in full bloom and turns square-metre-sized patches of grass azure blue, it is well visited by bumblebees and other wild bees. Protecting this plant is good for these insects, so I tolerate its inflorescences turning into brown withered cones that tower over the grass.

I also accept the groups of withered dog daisies. I love these white-petalled stars with their large, yolk-yellow centres — and so do some beautiful beetles. They are spared the first mow, as are some patches of tall grass, and any areas that are full of the delicate, cloudy-white and sky-blue blooms of speedwell, or which are home to groups of campions. And, and, and … There is so much to consider and to preserve. My objective is to allow for a variety of plants that are pleasing to the eye.

In my garden, the lawnmower must not create conditions akin to an English cricket ground, where there is nothing but short-shorn green grass. That effect could be more easily achieved with AstroTurf. In my attempts to allow for and preserve a diversity of plants, I have had to make many compromises. The requirements of the different species are too varied for me to be able to do justice to anywhere near all of them, but many benefit from moderate, mosaic-like mowing. I only get to glimpse a portion of the garden's diversity, for many species live their lives at night or keep themselves as camouflaged as they can. The butterflies that appear during the day give me an indication of the vast number of winged creatures that must be active at night.

When I allow myself an idle hour simply to watch the activity in the garden, I appreciate the fruits of my labour. In doing so, I become aware, with complete clarity, that everything I do in the garden has consequences, causes changes, and triggers counter-reactions. I cannot take all those complex relationships and interactions into consideration because I do not understand them as a whole. But I feel involved in the happenings, and from that I draw great joy.

Roses and Palms

I am in love with my roses. Flowering from June to December, they don't resent my poor knowledge of rose care. Sometimes, I think they are glad that I don't fuss over them too much, and are perhaps all the more splendid because of it. That is often the case in gardens; too much human influence creates stiffness, making plants appear formal and unnatural.

It is shocking that I, of all people, as a Japanese woman, could write such a thing — it is common knowledge that uncontrolled growth is not permitted in Japanese gardens. And that's not even considering the cultivation of bonsai! Not even the harshest diet of deprivation could make saplings grow into the minute tree forms that secateurs can create. Although it might seem as though this way of describing Japanese horticulture is clichéd, these are nevertheless widespread forms of artistic design used in small gardens in Japan.

My vegetable patch could pass as a mini allotment. The decorative section of the garden in front of the house where flowers and bushes grow could, from an ant's perspective, be described as castle grounds. My roses are the plants I see most frequently because of their placement in front of my living-room window; I have to look over them to see the rest of the garden. Gazing at their perfectly symmetrical flowers, with petals of velvety, resplendent, sultry red, delicate pink, yellow deepening from ivory in the centre to lemon on the tips, or with vibrantly coloured edges, I drift away into memories of my childhood and youth in Japan.

My grandparents and great-grandparents had artistically designed gardens in Japan. I cannot recall any particular details, but I do know that my great-uncle's garden contained a large collection of palms. As a small private park, it was situated on top of a hill on the edge of town. Palms of the most varied species and shapes were arranged so that they framed a vista of the vast Sakurajima volcano. It was a living landscape painting of sublime beauty, a far cry from bonsai or Zen gardens.

My great-uncle kept tender tropical palms along with ferns in a crystalline greenhouse that didn't look out of place in the garden. The bay in front of the volcano glistened blue, and beyond it there was a hint of the distant ocean. This view was framed by delicate green, either by palm fronds emanating from gently curved, graceful trunks of consistent thickness, or by huge leaves that rose from the bright-green manicured lawn like frozen fountains. The wind that blew through the garden occasionally caused them to sway as if to an inaudible melody. As a child, the awe I felt on each visit probably already resembled the beginnings of a meditation, directed towards the essence of plants and their forms. I imagine that my great-uncle would have been a fantastic Zen master. Maybe he even sensed my awe and saw in it the nascent buds of Zen.

The type of design that directs your eye into the distance is known as *shakkei*, or 'borrowed scenery'. For me, roses are the opposite of scenery; your eyes are drawn to their beauty above all else. Their flowers seem to surpass the forms and colours achieved in the rest of nature. I just want to delve into them, drink in their scent, and act like the shiny, emerald-green rose chafer, which burrows itself with unfettered desire into the heart of the rose. Diving into the rose petals, the beetle appears to forget both itself and the world. Sometimes, on mornings that follow cool nights, I find these beetles asleep inside the flowers. They could hardly ask for a better shelter for the night. Although, perhaps I am looking at the flowers through rose-tinted spectacles? After all, dung beetles, close relatives of the rose chafer, have other preferences: a sun-dried cowpat, for instance.

For me, the roses separate two worlds of contemplation. Immersion in their beauty functions as a pathway inward. But beyond them, outside, is a vast external world. My great-uncle's palm garden taught me about perspective in a way no other garden has. Looking at the view induced the greatest pleasure and the deepest calm as it channelled your gaze through an avenue of dark-green palm fronds and plants towards the volcano and eternity. Everything in sight formed one single entity, from the greenhouse through the garden to the occasionally misty mountains.

The scene had to be taken in from a sitting position. You could not linger for long enough to appreciate it fully if you were standing. Concentrating on the view, the image would develop a profound harmony, a feeling that transcended the garden and moved inwards. Slowly walking through the garden was not enough to achieve this feeling.

Our sitting positions were corrected if they had not been properly assumed. The height of our eyes and the position of our bodies had to be right. Children were gently but firmly guided until everything was perfect. Then the calm could unfold. Our senses opened up and we could begin to feel more strongly the emotions that our surroundings generated in us. Admonishments changed to praise. The tableau appeared to speak. Poise was the answer. It taught us the qualities we should uphold even once we had left the garden: reservation, attention, and prudence. Without understanding it, we children absorbed what the garden taught us as if it were an elder, one who was always good and benevolent. Above all, we learnt that this was more than just scenery; it was alive. I was taught that nature is a teacher.

Trees, shrubs, open areas, stones, flowers, small ponds, and babbling brooks represent nature — constant, yet forever changing. The seasons cloak gardens in different guises. In my grandparents' and great-grandparents' gardens, I experienced the diversity of nature. Every garden may be different, but they are all still gardens: places in which to find yourself, relax, and reflect until all thinking becomes lost in itself. Stone lanterns, tiny bridges over small streams, and red autumn acer leaves on dark mossy lawns become places that hold the eye, where senses replace thought.

Flowers are less important in Japanese gardens. They can convey the season in the way an *ikebana* arrangement does, or they can represent a certain event. As schoolgirls we covered the schoolyard with a carpet of rose petals in May because we had learnt that it was a tradition at

Assumption Day processions in Europe. Although, that was the only Christian custom we took part in, as culture in my homeland is more influenced by Buddhism.

Occasionally, in European gardens, roses seem almost to push themselves into the foreground with their beauty and draw attention away from the rest of the garden. Just like my roses, which, in my opinion, look distinct from the other plants — art versus nature. I like them for that very reason.

I have repeatedly suffered scratches when being forced to prune them. Drops of blood would cling to their thorns until the next rain — or until an insect found them and licked them off. The roses flower until winter and beyond if there is no frost in December. On sunny winter days, I find wispy flies with black rings around their flat abdomens on the roses; they are hoverflies whose larvae prey on aphids. How they always manage to find the last rose of winter, clinging to life despite being so out of season, is a mystery to me. I am in awe of these insects, as they are hardier than the roses. The flowers will fall victim to frosts whereas the small hoverflies, known as marmalade flies, survive. There is an entire world of insects between them and the bronzed rose chafers, but the rose unites them and numerous other creatures, too. I think that is amazing.

I would love to know where my roses originate from, but with the multitude of cultivars and crossed species that exists, I don't even want to attempt to trace their heritage. I can live with their secret. I get enough joy from seeing their modest relatives flower at the end of May or in June: the light-pink dog roses and the slightly smaller, white field rose. At first, I struggled to recognise them as 'roses' at all. The thorns on their branches were more telling than their flowers, which consist of just five flat discoid petals. As a result, they bear more resemblance to pink apple blossom and white pear blossom than to large, round garden roses, who shed their abundance of petals when it rains.

In a single day, a garden rose can morph into a fist-sized, browning clump, while the petals of apple and pear blossom, as well as those of the dog and field roses, resist the rain for much longer. I must accept that evanescence is the price of beauty. Apple and pear trees are rosaceous plants, meaning they actually belong to the same family as wild roses and my garden roses. However, their simple flowers serve only to attract bees and other pollinators until they have been pollinated so they can develop into fruits: into apples, pears, and rosehips.

My apple trees are the opposite of the roses in front of my living-room window; they are also positioned opposite the roses, but still are close to the house. So close that I can watch the development of their blossom and fruit. Being able to watch them so closely also means I often fear for them. It is unfortunately rare for weather conditions to allow them to produce an abundant harvest of delicious apples. Late frosts may damage the blossom and leave the trees unable to re-bloom. Roses can tolerate their flowers being cut off — they just grow new ones that are all the more sumptuous. This is an impossible feat for apple trees.

If the tree has produced lots of blossom, many little apples will fall to the ground, either because there has been a lack of bees and my pollination attempts were unsuccessful, or because too many have developed, and the small trees are opportunely shedding the burden of growing too much fruit. Apples can also be afflicted by codling moths, becoming 'maggoty', and scabs can form on the fruits. In the worst cases, trees can be plagued with fire blight, which causes the tips of their shoots to turn black and drop off.

In the event that all goes unusually well, like in the uniquely wonderful summer of 2018, the little trees buckle under the sheer weight of their apples. Because they all look so impeccably beautiful, I never want to remove the excess fruit, even though it will help to improve the quality of the apples that are left. The contrast between apple trees and roses, both rosaceous plants, illustrates how the most different plants can develop from the same starting conditions. From one year to the next, the apple trees fluctuate between feasting and famine, and the less I intervene, the more exaggerated this fluctuation is. On their own, they cannot produce even a moderate harvest.

The roses can keep blooming and blooming for evermore, provided the weather conditions are suitable. They put up with being staked and pruned, and do not give up. Even aphids don't affect them, which is good, because the battle I am conducting against those sticky suckers on the hibiscus right next to the roses is almost driving me to despair. I struggle year after year without the prospect of a final victory.

Aphids also infest the apple trees' new shoots. Whatever the unfavourable weather, 'apple maggots', and scabs have not managed to spoil, the aphids do. 'Poor apples,' I sometimes groan, as I cut back the rosebushes so that they will bloom again, beautifully and magnificently, throughout summer and autumn, and into the winter.

Roses can make one of the finest gifts. In 1961, a new, single-coloured, light-carmine English rose was given the name 'Princess Michiko' as a sign of friendship between Great Britain and Japan. At the time, Michiko was still a princess. When she became the empress in 1991 (until 2019, when Akihito, the 125th emperor, abdicated), the British royal family dedicated another rose to her: the exceptionally delicate, creamy, pale-pink 'Empress Michiko'. Honorific gifts of this kind come with an obligation of attentive care; the expectation is that they should live for a long time. However, even the most beautiful roses are perishable. This expectation does not really align with the teachings of Zen. Instead, Zen can be found in the transient elegance of the rose and the other plants in the garden. When thinking about all their beauty, I sense the wonderful harmony of nature, at least a little.

Potatoes

I enjoy eating potatoes: pan-fried potatoes, jacket potatoes, potato salad, chips, mashed potatoes, or even potatoes topped with cheese. On early shopping trips in Germany, I had to learn what 'waxy' and 'floury' meant. Floury potatoes have much more starch, and go fluffy when cooked, while waxy potatoes have less starch, making them harder and better for boiling. As I experimented with different potato recipes, I thought a lot about the dishes I would make, and about eating them, but I didn't think about the potatoes themselves. The notion of growing them myself was as foreign to me as planting rice in my garden in Germany, although I do still enjoy eating rice outside of Japan.

A dream changed all this: I had dug up beautiful and surprisingly delicious potatoes from the garden. I was sweating because they were so big and the soil that I had to sieve to reveal them was heavy. I noted with surprise that slugs had not feasted on them. Without a doubt, it was a desire to grow potatoes that must have given birth to this dream.

In the supermarket, I often had to choose between many different varieties of potato, none of which I knew or had any way of judging. The only difference between them seemed to be how well washed they were. At the weekly market, the vendors only extolled the virtues of their selection of potatoes. They were almost always pleasant, but none of their potatoes were terribly special. Occasionally, I was given a particularly good one 'to try', but, unfortunately, when it came to lunch, those potatoes would disappear among the other pan-fried ones; none of them had a distinctive taste. I also kept forgetting the names of the many varieties, and even when I did remember, their names didn't reveal anything about their taste or any of their specific qualities.

Since I grew lettuce in the garden and defended it from snails, caterpillars, and all other lovers of 'true organic food', growing potatoes became the next obvious choice. I would grow the potatoes whose flavour I particularly liked. I also didn't want to continue to prepare sushi or curried rice every day, and the idea of making chips from my own harvest was tempting. However, I should have noted the warning my dream had given me about the true laboriousness of the task I was about to undertake.

In the morning, as I contemplated the dream that had stuck in my head with such an unusual amount of detail, a phrase came to mind. It was a phrase that I had heard many times in the German countryside but, for a long time, didn't understand: 'The dumbest farmers have the biggest potatoes!' A rough translation would be: 'Being clever does not guarantee success.'

I planted a mini potato field right next to the lettuces, where they would get the full morning sun and shade from the house in the afternoon. My husband thought the soil wasn't sandy enough, so he brought a couple of buckets of the finest sand he could find up from the river to improve the earth for potato growing. Apparently, they like poor soil, which surprised me, because you would think they would need lots of nutrients to form large tubers. I was even more surprised at how their less-than-impressive leaves, which grow throughout the summer, can somehow provide a haul of large potatoes.

As I waited for the crop to ripen for harvest, the lettuce kept me busy. If I successfully protected them against snails, I would have more lettuce than even the healthiest of people could eat. If the snails ate them, I would have to buy lettuce at the supermarket or weekly farmers' market. I hoped that it would be different with the potatoes. They would be free to grow as abundantly as they could, as we wouldn't have to eat them straight away, while still fresh. Nevertheless, my limited experience in growing potatoes put my patience to the test. I knew that under no circumstances should I lift the first potatoes too early. Yet, nobody could tell me whether it was still too early or whether it was time to harvest. If I asked at the market, I was met with counter-questions: what variety were they, and when did I plant them? Nobody had mentioned that I needed to do a kind of account-keeping when planting my potatoes. I was heartened to learn that it also depended on the position of the potatoes in the garden, the amount of shade, soil type, and how often they were watered.

A good indicator is the appearance of the potato leaves. Mine had looked good throughout the summer, until I discovered a beetle sitting upon the leaves: its half-spherical form and the eye-catching yellow and black stripes running lengthwise up its body immediately, frustratingly, identifying it as a potato beetle. I had become acquainted with this insect under very different, rather unusual circumstances, namely sitting on deadly nightshade in the middle of a large forest. I had now found several of them eating my potato leaves. Rather unenthusiastically, in my opinion, but eating them nonetheless.

Spotting potato beetle larvae feeding on deadly nightshade is actually not as peculiar as it might seem. This plant, like the potato, is part of the nightshade family, all of which are more or less poisonous; the majority of them more rather than less so. Potato beetles ingest poison from the nightshade, making them toxic to birds that might want to eat them. Their distinct yellow and black stripes serve as a warning to those birds. This means that, rather than having to fly off quickly to safety, they can afford to remain sitting sluggishly. It is alien to the beetle and larvae world that we might not seek to eat them but still want to kill them. This is not only true for the potato beetle — which, as I learnt, originated in America, just like the potato plant — the same goes for other creatures that survive by eating potato leaves.

Under certain circumstances, in a small garden, creatures from the Old and New World can meet on this foliage. Just like my husband, from Bavaria, and I, a Japanese woman, do when we eat these potatoes. Globalisation on a plate. Unfortunately, my potatoes have not yet done me the favour of harbouring the African creature that I would like to find on their leaves: the death's-head hawk-moth. Almost every year, when the weather conditions are favourable, these mighty moths fly over the Alps from Africa in search of German potatoes. The females lay their eggs on the sprouting leaves; not too many and not too close together. The caterpillars become very big and need a corresponding amount of food. When they are ready to pupate, they become the size of small sausages. Some of the caterpillars are a gaudy yellow and are covered in diagonal stripes that range from blue to light violet, while others are brown like wilted potato leaves. They are inedible due to the poison they collect in their bodies through their food. Partridges, pheasants, and other farmland birds immediately recognise that they are not to be eaten, or learn it after their first attempt.

Since the soil in a potato patch is usually light and free of other plants, fully grown death's-head hawk-moth caterpillars only need to dig a small hole in which to pupate. The caterpillar stays enclosed in a mahogany-coloured chrysalis until its transformation into a moth is complete, and it can hatch. They emerge between the end of September and mid-October, provided that the summer has been warm enough. This giant among moths hatches, crawls out of its hole, and climbs a little up the potato leaves. It waits there a while until its wings have fully unfolded and hardened. At dusk, if the weather is favourable, it will begin its flight south over the Alps and across the ocean, back to Africa, like a migratory bird.

I am happy to sacrifice my potato leaves for such a wonder from the world of butterflies and moths. Since potato harvesting has become automated and fields are sprayed with fungicides and pesticides, the death's-head hawk-moth has become a rarity. Its chances for survival reside in the garden, provided no poison has been used and potatoes are lovingly lifted from the ground, not mechanically harvested. After the summer of 2018, a beekeeper brought us a death's-head hawk-moth that was almost unrecognisable at first glance. It had invaded a beehive and gorged itself on honey. When the bees discovered it, they covered it in wax and embalmed it. The beekeeper found it, mummified. Unfortunately, none of its relatives paid my garden a visit in that legendary summer. I would have happily given the hatched moths honey as fuel for their long flight over the mountains, sea, and deserts.

My potato leaves withered anyway without being nibbled too much by potato beetles, and not at all by death's-head hawk-moth caterpillars. Thanks to the warm and dry summer weather, there was no potato blight.

When the potato leaves looked ready for the compost bin, I deduced that it must be the right time to lift them. I picked a day with fine autumn weather, which would make any possible disappointment more bearable, had my first attempt at growing potatoes been a failure. However, what I harvested were, in my opinion, the biggest and most beautiful potatoes ... Of course they tasted better than any I had ever bought — my taste buds expected that they would, after all the months of effort. They had only been fertilised occasionally with nettle manure and so were completely organic. My husband agreed that they were objectively exquisite, but warned against leaving them in the light where they would turn green and poisonous. Luckily, they didn't have the chance to do that with me around; with the addition of sweet and sour cream, salt and pepper, and a squeeze of lemon, my harvest was magicked into a very tasty Lower Bavarian 'potato spread'. Served on coarse rye bread, it was eaten far quicker than I could produce it. Since then, I have been planting potatoes every year on a significantly larger patch and don't worry whether they will produce a crop or not. I am still hoping for a visit from the death's-head hawk-moth.

Tomatoes

I was already familiar with tomatoes in Japan, where we call them *tomato* or トマト. I learnt at some point that this is not a Japanese word; instead, it is derived from the old Mexican word *tomatl*. We Japanese adopted the name from the Americans. In my youth, I enjoyed eating the bright-red, aromatic tomatoes that grew on the volcanic earth of Japan's southern island. In contrast, German supermarket tomatoes are hard and tasteless. When I decided to grow some myself, tomatoes became more than just a fruit — a challenge to master.

My first question was which variety I should grow. At first, I was surprised to discover that there were different varieties. I thought they had all long since been done away with by EU legislation, because perfectly formed, shiny, round, standard, uniformly sized tomatoes were all that was on offer in supermarkets. The vibrant, glossy red was an attempt to compensate for the lack of flavour. This situation seemed Japanese to me. In Japan, we say that you eat with your eyes, and often that is true; however, striving for the most perfect-looking fruit can sometimes lead to less flavour. The main goal is uniformity and an attractive appearance; such fruits can get away with less taste. Tomatoes such as these are seasoned; in a salad, they simply get an extra dash of vinegar or even a dressing.

Tasteless EU-standardised tomatoes are naturally not what I aspired to grow in my garden. They wouldn't be worth the effort, nor would they satisfy my expectations — I would never be able to grow perfectly round, bright-red tomatoes. Cocktail or cherry tomatoes would be easier to grow, or even the tomatoes that I had enjoyed on Lake Neusiedl in Austria. Those tomatoes deserved the name they had been given: love apples! What a lovely name; it just invites you to take a bite.

I was attracted to tomatoes for another reason as well: they are considered to be easy to grow. 'It'll work straight away,' I was told by the friendly vegetable seller at the weekly market where I buy seasonal fruit and vegetables. 'I'll bring you some seedlings,' the eighty-five-year-old promised. 'They'll grow well.' She brought the little plants to my house. As I had always liked the taste of her tomatoes, I felt obliged to give them a go myself.

They brought to mind an image: Hermann Hesse carefully tending his staked and supported tomato plants, the great German poet visibly proud of his tomatoes. He said that his plants, laden with love apples, stood beautifully in straight rows, juicy and dripping with foliage. He also candidly advised to cover all the roots with moist, light garden peat, into which he mixed a small amount of chemical fertiliser. Instantly sobered by this advice, my wonderful vision deflated. I wanted to use neither peat nor chemical fertilisers. The moorlands need the remaining peat. These landscapes have been exploited over the centuries and have almost vanished completely. What little is left should not be used for tomatoes. That much was clear to me. A hundred years ago, it may have been (somewhat) different. I convinced myself that if Hermann Hesse were alive today, he would definitely think and act in a more environmentally friendly manner. But how am I to perform the trick of growing seductively red and aromatic tomatoes, without the use of a chemical fertiliser? Fertiliser would only make them look good on the outside, anyway; the inside would remain tasteless. Then, something began to dawn on me. Something that I should address both in the garden and beyond, in a more far-reaching and occasionally gloomy way: what brings about growth and encourages life to thrive?

The biggest, juiciest, and sweetest radishes in the world grow in my homeland. That is no exaggeration, not even when taking into account that we tend to glorify things from home — they become our reference for anything new and different. No, in all honesty, these radishes can get so big that you can hardly carry them. A single radish could feed a whole beer tent! There are enough photos on the internet as evidence. And their growth is not fuelled by multi-purpose sprays with chemical fertiliser and growth hormones in them. Volcanic earth brought about this miracle of growth all on its own. The soil is crucial — it's a kind of soil that we don't have in Germany, and definitely not in my garden. The earth that is actually available in my garden reveals its quality through the mossy lawn that covers it, which, at best, after spring rainfall, gives the impression of needing to be mowed. Still, it can't be completely devoid of quality, as flowers do manage to bloom in it, many flowers.

I banished any thoughts I had about flowers, which should continue to grow and blossom even in poor soil, in favour of tomatoes. My tomatoes would need the best of the best: organic soil enriched with home-made compost. In a standard compost bin, our organic kitchen and garden waste turns into great compost. That fact is proven by the fat rose chafer grubs that live in it. Their existence and appearance take some getting used to, but the magnificent metallic-green beetles they grow into are worth it. My tomatoes should grow at least as well as their larvae do in the compost. The organic waste that breaks down to form the compost comes from organic vegetables, so I assume it is also free of any environmental poisons. Otherwise, developing rose chafers, worms, and, unfortunately, slugs would not thrive as well as they do now. Now, all the goodness from the compost will be used to enrich the soil and benefit my tomatoes.

The initially weedy-looking plants actually grew superbly; they literally shot up. Placing them against the south-east-facing house wall exposed them to the warmth of the sun from morning until late afternoon and did them good. However, I needed to water the pots and troughs in which I had planted them regularly and plentifully. Giving them water became a necessary daily task. Delighted by their fast growth, I gave them company in the form of pepper and lettuce plants growing in pots. I also let a morning glory grow up the house wall alongside the tomato plants.

I imagined the beauty to come when, in mid- and late summer, their large trumpet flowers would open up over the reddening tomatoes. Thin bamboo sticks, intended to allow the tomato plants to bear heavy fruits, could also be used by the morning glory as a climbing aid. It could reach upwards without squeezing out the tomatoes. Week to week, with growing satisfaction, I watched my handiwork visibly thriving. However, occasionally I had the creeping suspicion that the plants didn't look particularly strong. To put it bluntly, as time went on, they looked more and more puny.

On top of my growing worry, I got my first big shock: one morning, I noticed a pale-reddish, slimy lump in one of the pots. It was easy to spot because the fist-sized form had a disturbing likeness to fresh vomit. It appeared to be spilling over the top of the pot. Had a cat been sick? On closer inspection, that seemed unlikely. It couldn't have been from a hedgehog, which would have had difficulty climbing into the pot. Birds were out of the question as well. Confused, I called for my husband to show him the pink, porridge-like lumps. 'That's a slime fungus that has formed a fruiting body,' he curtly diagnosed. Explaining further, he added, 'It is not a fungus in the normal sense; slime fungus is completely different. They live as tiny single cells in the earth, are invisible to the naked eye, and are similar to amoebae. They pick their own time to come together to form a frame, a fruiting body where spores are formed. They are then spread by the wind, water, or animals, just like other fungi.'

Even though it had been identified, I still didn't understand it. Knowing that it was slime fungus that had formed this strange fruiting body in my tomato pots did nothing to calm me at all. What on earth was slime fungus doing in my tomato soil? I wanted to harvest flavoursome, glossy red love apples, not to watch an unappetising slime fungus reproducing. Where did their spores end up? Did identifying it as a slime fungus fruiting body tell us whether it would be good or bad for my tomato harvest?

My husband professed that he didn't know what effect slime fungus in the soil would have on the formation of tomatoes, as he had no experience in the matter. Research on the internet only revealed that the slime fungus in my tomato pots was small compared to what could have developed under more favourable conditions; what could have erupted as pink pulp towards the path or climbing up the house wall. I couldn't find anything about whether it harmed vegetables.

After this less-than-fruitful research, I discovered that the disgusting slime fungus had also formed in the lettuces. I grow salad leaves in pots, keeping the plants off the ground to protect against nightly slug attacks. My lettuce had not been nibbled by slugs, but it now had slime fungus cosying up to it. That was very frustrating. I could no longer suppress the realisation that organic earth and compost are full of life, and that at the beginning, you don't know what kind of life they hold. It reveals itself when it chooses and is usually quite a surprise.

A few dry, hot early-summer days followed by torrential rain got rid of the slime fungus. Had a grey, almost-white crust not clung to the tops of the pots afterwards, I would have thought it had been a delusion, a figment of my imagination arising from the over-eagerness with which I had approached tomato cultivation in my garden. At least it wasn't as bad as I had feared it might be when I first discovered it.

It was now the start of midsummer and the garden demanded that I focused on other tasks. The tomatoes still needed to be watered regularly, but when I did this, all I noticed was that they were growing well. Almost too much, I thought, as they reached one and a half to two metres in height. My fears that they had grown too high were put to rest when they started producing an abundance of flowers. I thought their small, yellow, star-shaped blossoms were cute, but they seemed far too delicate to grow into fist-sized tomatoes.

119

Although I saw bees visiting my flowers, hanging upside down to work, I didn't want to leave pollinating the flowers to the bees or to chance. With devotion, I tried to pollinate them myself by gently touching the flowers with my fingers and a brush. The bees weren't appearing frequently enough to undertake all the work themselves. A beekeeper acquaintance told us that some apiarists had now given up beekeeping because their hives had been so heavily infected with varroa mites and Nosema disease. Furthermore, they had been forced to give their bees additional food in autumn, and sometimes even in summer, because they could no longer find enough flowers. If there weren't enough bees to do it, I would bring my flowering tomato plants to fruit myself.

I watched with excitement as, week by week, the small green balls, which at first were barely recognisable as the fruits they were to become, gained a tomato shape, grew bigger, and gradually changed colour from a fine yellow shade to a typical tomato red. Some of them deviated from their usual spherical shape and became oval, like miniature melons. They ripened and turned red everywhere except for the tips. The bottom, which pointed to the ground, didn't become round as would be expected. Instead, they were stumpy and a black brown. They looked as if they had been cut off and were rotten.

Some of my tomatoes — fortunately, only the variety that formed relatively large, cylindrical fruits — were suffering from an unusual, lesser-known deficiency. It caused the downward-pointing end of the fruit to harden, turn black, and rot. It happened in mid-June, during a spell of the best possible tomato weather. I had watered them plenty, so it was certainly not due to a lack of water, and they couldn't have overheated because the plants were in the shade.

Unfortunately, what they actually lacked was the 'small amount of chemical fertiliser' Hermann Hesse had written about. They were suffering from a mineral deficiency, a deficiency of magnesium and potassium, or some other important mineral nutrient, maybe even just trace amounts of it. The ripening tomatoes, whose lower thirds had turned black, forced me to rethink my organic earth and compost mix — I had to add additional nutrients to it. The tomatoes needed more than the soil could provide.

Now, I understood why I'd occasionally had the impression that the leaves of my tomato plants looked puny. What satisfied the lettuce, revealing itself in the vegetable's growth and flavour, was simply not enough for tomato plants that grew up to two metres high and flowered abundantly. Nettle manure was needed to correct the deficiency. And it did. The blossom-end rot disappeared, and the tomatoes, large and small, were now growing magnificently. Towards the end of August, we had so many of them that we barely managed to eat them while they were still aromatic and fresh.

The morning glory thrived beside the tomatoes. It climbed high, and one tendril reached the tilted bathroom window. As if exploring, it stretched the tip of its tendril inside. From it, a couple of leaves grew as if they were one of my wall ornaments, and even a few flowers developed and unfolded. I couldn't have displayed them any more beautifully in an *ikebana* arrangement if I had tried.

However, soon some of the heart-shaped, lush leaves started to look a little damaged. Small, cylindrical, black crumbs collected beneath them on the windowsill. I searched the leaves but found nothing. Seemingly, a caterpillar was visiting the tips of the morning glory at night. I imagined it climbing the house wall to get there. My husband couldn't believe this and took a look himself. He found the caterpillar. It looked like a thick morning glory stem or a leaf's midrib, which enabled it to conceal itself. 'It's the caterpillar of an owlet moth,' he explained. 'Let's wait until it pupates. The morning glory has enough leaves. Once the caterpillar is ready to pupate, it'll stop eating. We just need to check in the morning whether fresh crumbs have fallen overnight.'

Since the tendril no longer had any buds anyway, I accepted his suggestion, although not without some hesitation. I checked every morning to see if there were crumbs in order not to miss the crucial moment. And I didn't miss it, even though I hadn't always remembered to count the crumbs. The caterpillar, which had become plump and ready to pupate, sat stretched out on the underside of a leaf and did not move. Carefully, we removed it and the surrounding leaves, and placed them in a glass container covered with gauze. The following night, it pupated. About three weeks later, like in the story of *The Very Hungry Caterpillar*, a beautiful butterfly was sitting in the glass. And what a beauty it was! It was a moth with which my husband was unfamiliar, and so he challenged experts to identify it. Unbelievably, it was a golden twin-spot, which is native to South-East Asia. Its hatching signalled the end of the tomato year. The final carmine-red tomatoes were hanging on the bent, wispy side shoots of the visibly perishing plants. My first tomatoes had been a complete success and had taught me a great deal. Since then, I have grown all our tomatoes myself.

Cabbages

I believe that sauerkraut is healthy, provided you eat it in moderation. I also like the taste of it. The amount is crucial, that much is clear. But what is the right amount? When I ask for 150 grams at the weekly market, I am given a quarter of a kilo at least, if not 300 grams, and I'm charged for the pleasure. The seller, who is usually very nice, looks at me as if I were still a small child. Does the amount I request not equate to a normal serving of this superfood? That my stomach grumbles after eating only half a portion is clearly supposed to be part of its charm. It demonstrates its effect. A small portion is enough for my wellbeing and vitamin intake.

I didn't intend to replace sauerkraut in my diet when I decided to plant white cabbage in the garden. I heard that to make sauerkraut you needed barrels, a cellar that was kept cool, and wellington boots to press the finely sliced cabbage together and bring it to fermentation. Our cellar was not suitable, nor could I imagine wanting to make a whole barrel of sauerkraut, when half a kilo was already much too much for me. On the other hand, I was sure I would be able to acquire a taste for beautifully round cabbage heads. What's more, my friendly vegetable seller pointed out that cabbages are just as easy to grow as tomatoes, actually even easier, because no care is required to ensure their flowers blossom and are pollinated, and you don't have to give them anything to climb up.

She added that a cabbage becomes a cabbage head entirely on its own; you don't need to shape the leaves. You can just let the plants do their thing. In the hot and dry midsummer weather they only need occasional watering; the only thing you need to be careful of is not to drown them. Cabbage is very easy. That is why it grows regionally as a field crop. The cabbage heads look impressive when they're harvested: full wagon-loads of them, each cabbage head bigger than a football, and much heavier. However, I should have thought about why the tiny plants cost next to nothing.

I bought a dozen of the waxy, light-green plants and another dozen of the reddish-blue ones. They were to grow into white and red cabbages. Although my small, purple-toned plants looked somewhat weak, I was sure that they would become proper red cabbages with firm heads. Strangely, the others, which were to become white cabbages, turned increasingly green. I could not imagine how and why a head would form out of these normal, upstanding leaves. My imagination struggled even more when the little plants really started to grow: their leaves projected outwards instead of towards the centre. At this point the summer was still young, and the days long. I read that as the days grew shorter, the leaves would bend inwards and form a ball. They must do, because for years I had been buying cabbage heads at the local market or in shops that were sizes suited to my needs: small, manageable specimens, not giant cabbage heads that I could hardly lift.

I could not uncover the secret of how they formed their heads. When I asked friends and acquaintances, they either declared, 'That's just how it is,' or they shrugged their shoulders and said, 'I don't know.' I thought about this problem more and more; something must make the cabbage plants bend their growing leaves inwards until the innermost leaves have no space at all, and are pressed together, no longer able to unfold properly. These leaves have the appearance of shallow bowls that have been stuck on to the plant.

The way a cabbage head develops confused me — they direct their strength inwardly in a way reminiscent of a kind of meditation: when deep in meditation, you can try to turn your focus inwards and concentrate on and be aware of yourself, your body, and your senses; the leaves curling up to form cabbage heads are also concentrating. The thought should have made me laugh, because comparing cabbage heads and meditation is so absurd. Nevertheless, I could not get these thoughts out of my head, because nobody could tell me why it happens and what forces are at work.

Finding holes in the leaves distracted me from my (pseudo) philosophical thoughts about cabbages. The plants had developed well, were strong, and had spread their leaves wide. However, I suddenly realised that there were irregularly shaped holes in their leaves. Without a doubt, some creatures were eating my cabbages. No sooner had I discovered the holes than I knew which enemy was at work. The large, slimy slugs that left trails over the beds at night had to be the culprits, if only because I could not stand them.

The slugs also roamed during the day when the weather was wet. They were unmissable, as they appeared in numbers that no normal garden could withstand and no hedgehog, however hungry, could eat. I immediately took action. I used beer to try to keep these ravenous creatures away from my young cabbage plants and the kohlrabi plants that I was growing in the bed next to them. The slugs clearly preferred the kohlrabi, maybe because they were more tender than the cabbages. Nevertheless, I didn't want to share either of them with the slugs.

In the evening, I placed wonderfully scented, shallow bowls of dark beer sweetened with honey around the cabbage plants. The brew smelt so good that it just had to work. What slug could resist such temptation? I didn't spend much time wondering whether a hedgehog might get drunk if it slurped up the sweet beer, because we hadn't had any hedgehogs in our garden yet that year. The next morning, my disappointment was huge. Despite the mild night, only one slug had been to my bar, and it did not appear to be under the influence. It wouldn't have enraged me as much if the holes in the cabbage leaves hadn't increased in size and spread to new places. But I couldn't find any slugs or snails on the plants or even close to them. I could find lots of them in the compost and, unfortunately, some lingering close to my ripening strawberries.

To make matters worse, my dog, who had noticed my confused searching, also started hunting. He rummaged through the cabbage patch until his nose looked like the snout of a wild boar. He wanted to be praised for his efforts, something I found difficult, as the bed now also looked like a wild boar had ploughed through it. He had dug out several cabbage plants, most likely because he didn't appreciate their smell. I replanted them, told the dog that there was nothing more to do here, and took him back into the house with me.

I knew that freshly dug earth was attractive to dogs; something could be buried in it, like an old bone. A walk through the woods would be needed to distract him. Breathing in the forest air would also help me to clear my head and develop a new strategy to protect the cabbages. It would have to be a completely different strategy to the last, as that afternoon I discovered the real culprit: the cabbage white butterfly caterpillar. It wasn't slugs that had attacked my cabbage plants but little hungry caterpillars.

I carefully picked these caterpillars off all the plants, but I could see that wasn't going to be enough. Several cabbage white butterflies danced through the garden. With the aid of a butterfly book, my suspicions grew. The broad, dark-brown wingtips and the pair of black spots on their forewings revealed them to be the large cabbage whites. This butterfly has a particular penchant for cabbage. It's more delicate but otherwise very similar in appearance to its cousin, the small cabbage white, which is not as fussy.

At the time, I was relatively uninterested in their differences. Whether they were large or small cabbage whites, they were without doubt searching for small plants upon which they could lay their eggs. These plants would have to smell right, i.e. of cabbage. My cabbage plants fitted the bill. I could not change their scent, but I could deter these creamy-white butterflies, which I suddenly admired a lot less, in a different way. I had thought of them as pretty, with their understated ivory beauty, sitting on the buddleja flowers drinking nectar. I no longer looked upon them kindly. How quickly things change! Furthermore, I had found a solution to stop their destruction of my cabbage plants.

During the spring, I had fenced off the entrance to the vegetable patch with roll-up mesh to stop my dog digging up or hiding something in beds I had just turned. I now placed this mesh over my cabbage patch, so that the cabbage whites would be locked out, but the plants would still benefit from sunlight and air. I was still able to water the plants through the zinc-coated mesh. I regarded my work with great satisfaction, even if my dog was of a different opinion. There were plenty of other corners in the garden where he could dig, but he much preferred digging in the freshly turned soil.

For a few days, there was nothing but pure sunshine; both outside, due to the most wonderful early-summer weather, and in my head, because I kept imagining how the cabbage whites would try and fail to get at my plants through the mesh. I watered them when they needed it, until a storm relieved me of this duty. The plants grew magnificently. The nibbled cabbage leaves turned yellow and bowed towards the ground. Soon they would be compost, as desired. Even the kohlrabi situation looked good. But not even a week had passed before I noticed that the cabbage whites had outsmarted me.

I discovered some yolk-yellow, grainy specks on one of the pretty white cabbage leaves. I didn't need a magnifying glass to identify them as around twenty eggs. Lustreless and spherical in form, they clung close together on the underside of the leaf, which was now visible from the side due to the powerful upward growth of the leaves. There was not just the one clutch — I found three more, with a combined total of over fifty eggs. They would have produced enough caterpillars to completely decimate all my cabbage and kohlrabi plants. Then, I noticed something else. In one corner, a female large cabbage white fluttered underneath the mesh. Her abdomen had become slim like the males, and her eggs clung to my little plants. I had no choice other than to squash these eggs. As with aphids, squashing them wasn't hard, but it was accompanied by more emotion.

The butterfly must have held her wings flat and at an angle in order to force her way under the mesh, which had not been laid evenly over the soil. I spared the female; she had done her job and, after laying her eggs, she would perish anyway. Birds wouldn't eat her. Cabbage whites protect themselves with the exact thing that makes their preferred vegetable so healthy for humans: the poisonous glucosinolates. When we eat cabbage, we ingest an amount that isn't dangerous to us, but is enough to kill bacteria — it cleanses our intestines. It is the dose that makes the poison.

Glucosinolates come with great benefits for cabbage whites and their caterpillars. The caterpillars store so much of them in their bodies that they taste bad to the majority of birds, and can even be poisonous, for instance if a parent bird were to feed one to their young. Stored glucosinolates are transferred from the caterpillars to the butterflies via the pupa, meaning that cabbage white butterflies also do not make for a tasty snack.

This is why these butterflies can afford to fly around so noticeably and slowly. I have only rarely seen one that had a small piece of its wing missing, a mark showing that a bird had nipped at it but was not able to catch it fully by the wings. These beak marks are more frequently found on butterflies that are not protected by poison or a foul taste. As they rarely have to fly away quickly from predators, cabbage whites can be caught by hand with a little skill and a slow approach. I put that into practice as I caught the female in my cabbage patch — and let her go.

So, my protective mesh was not butterfly-proof. It made me think: mesh can hold back the dog, but not fragile, delicate butterflies. I went to the nearest garden centre and asked for advice. No poison — I excluded that as an option from the outset, which did not make the search for the solution any easier. How could there be so many 'untreated', 'unsprayed', and 'organic' products offered at the market every week, when I couldn't even protect my dozen cabbage heads?

New traces of nibbling were visible on the leaves, even though I thought that I had destroyed all the cabbage white eggs. I patched up what I imagined could be used as entrance holes, but it didn't help. The minibeasts were beating me. If it had been midges or fleas, my failures would not have hit me as hard — but it was butterflies, of all insects. They appear to have been made only for beauty — this particular species is so sensitive that a brief touch is enough to damage the scales on their wings. To be outwitted by them insulted my honour and aggrieved my soul. I was unable to make any progress with my Zen exercises; on the contrary, my fight with the cabbage whites became the anti-Zen in my small garden project. I was unable to see them in a way similar to the famous poet Issa Kobayashi (1763–1827), who wrote the following haiku: 'Congratulations Issa ... you have survived to feed this year's mosquitoes.'

As bitterly poor as he was, at least he still had his blood. He had nothing else to offer, just blood for the mosquitoes.

Thinking of Issa's haiku calmed me a little. I remembered that the person at the garden centre had mumbled something about nets. That was logical: a finely woven net could be laid so close to the ground around the bed that even the butterflies would not be able to break in. My husband, taunting my obsession, placed a sign on the frame of the cabbage bed that bore the words, 'No entry for cabbage whites!' In response to my irritated, 'You with your insects!' he answered calmly, 'My insects were Brown China-mark water moths, not cabbage whites!'

The following day I replaced the mesh with a net that looked as if it were mosquito-proof and made watering the plants more difficult. I destroyed all the existing clutches of eggs and caterpillars, and the cabbage whites no longer had a chance of getting back in. Now, the cabbage plants could grow uneaten, but only dull light reached them. Another disadvantage was that I could no longer see exactly what was happening beyond the net. By now it was August, and the cabbage plants had started to form heads in that way I found so mysterious.

But despite my many efforts, I still spotted new nibble damage: large holes in the leaves that appeared black through the white net. Again, I had to accept defeat and ask my husband for advice. The shape of the hole assisted his diagnosis: 'Large yellow underwing.' It rendered me speechless. The large yellow underwing, which could not have been given a stranger name in German (*Hausmutter*, meaning 'house mother'), is a butterfly, but belongs to the owlet moth family. Moth enthusiasts call them *Noctua pronuba* because, as lepidopterists, they hardly ever call moths by their common names. They prefer to use their more inaccessible, secret scientific language. In this case, it worked at making them sound like experts, because while referring to *Noctua pronuba* sounds erudite, calling them 'large yellow underwings' or 'house mothers' sounds like baby talk.

So why, of all things, was I so fascinated by this owlet moth with a velvet-black stripe on its yellow underwings? When resting, it covers this stripe with its bark-coloured or rusty-brown front wings. Sitting on a tree trunk, the moth is barely visible, a testament to its bark camouflage. If you touch it in the way a bird that is testing if it could be edible might, its yellow underwings suddenly become visible, and the owlet moth flies away with a little jump.

The large yellow underwing moth is common. On summer nights, when lots of moths dance in the artificial light, it is often among them. I struggled to accept that this owlet moth was now my opponent. The reason we were now adversaries only became clear to me after I discovered more about the lifestyle of its caterpillars.

In mid- or late summer, they hatch from clutches of eggs laid by a female. A single clutch may contain hundreds of eggs, and a female can lay several clutches totalling approximately 2,000 to 3,000 eggs, something I learnt from a butterfly reference book. The freshly hatched caterpillars allow themselves to be carried on the breeze with a self-produced silk thread. Where they land is of little importance, because they can eat many different plants — although not my cabbages, as their leaves are far too thick to be eaten by the young caterpillars. However, later on, when they have grown larger, almost as long as my little finger, they can begin to munch on such plants.

These caterpillars had managed to break into my cabbage protection zone. During the day, they buried into the soil, only coming out to eat at night. I would never have guessed that a caterpillar would be able to burrow under my protective netting. I could never find any of them in daylight, no matter how carefully I searched the cabbage plants, on account of them hiding in the soil. Trying to find them would have been a hopeless undertaking. And so, I had to accept that large yellow underwing caterpillars would help themselves to a portion of my cabbage harvest. Either in late summer or next year, they would re-emerge in the form of butterflies with yellow, black-edged underwings. Fortunately, the cabbage heads, harvested early, showed that the caterpillars' feeding had been limited to the outer leaves, which were very tough anyway.

Not all of the plants survived. I harvested the kohlrabi too early, as I feared they would be eaten. What was left of them resembled only tattered stalks instead of leaves, but the root still tasted sweet and delicate. My red cabbage did not make it at all. I did get some beautiful, firm white cabbage heads, the last of which I harvested at the end of October; it weighed 650 grams. This green cannonball was a success, even if it wasn't record-breaking. The cabbage heads had grown to the exact small size that I wanted. I could easily handle and slice them. Of course, they were delicious: completely organic. Nothing in the taste revealed that the large yellow underwing had nibbled on them, too.

In the following years, I did things differently. Before planting, the freshly turned bed could not conceal any large yellow underwing caterpillars. And shortly after planting, I covered my cabbage bed with the mosquito-proof gauze. The patch now looked like a high-security prison, or at least a testing facility. Standing in rows, the cabbage plants were easily visible through the fine netting. Which meant that what happened next was also clearly visible: the plants were being eaten even more than the previous year, despite the bed being completely covered. Close to despair, I wanted to give up on growing cabbages; it was hopeless.

My investigation revealed something I could barely believe: small cabbage white caterpillars. How could they have got into my perfectly protected bed? Since the damage was already grave because the plants were still so small, we decided not to intervene. As an experiment. We theorised that the munching would eventually stop of its own accord, and it did over the course of the summer, but the process was frustratingly slow. The result was nearly forty perfectly formed small cabbage whites. The protection the net gave them meant the wind and rain were unable to harm the eggs and freshly hatched butterflies. My cabbage bed had become a breeding ground for cabbage whites. Clearly, they had been on the plants when I got them. This all contributed further to my increasing doubts about how 'organic' the organic products on offer at the market actually are.

Butterflies

I now have a love-hate relationship with butterflies. In this regard, I'm no different to many other people, surely even the majority of people, who want to enjoy a reasonable reward for their efforts. My internal conflict runs deep but, fortunately, it's not overwhelming, and I still delight in almost all butterflies. The exceptions being cabbage whites and the few moths whose caterpillars emerge from the soil even after I think I have fully protected my plants. I don't feel as exasperated with box tree moths — the two box trees that have been eaten by its 'worms' came from the garden centre anyway, and I didn't like them anywhere near as much as I like the Spanish lavender I planted in their place, next to the gazebo. It was a very successful replacement, especially for honeybees and bumblebees. Of course, I know that you cannot sacrifice all bushy box trees to the caterpillars of the pretty box tree moth with its shimmering, mother-of-pearl wings.

The situation with the box tree moth is actually more complicated than you might assume when reading about

them. The box tree isn't native to Bavaria. It originates
from the Mediterranean region and south-west Europe.
It is only since the sixteenth century that it has been
planted and valued as an ornamental bush here in Germany.
Another, also non-native, ornamental bush is of great
importance to butterflies in the garden: the butterfly
bush or *Buddleja davidii*. This plant was only introduced to
Europe at the end of the nineteenth century — not long
enough ago for it to have become as beloved as the box
tree. On the contrary, buddleja has been met with hostility.
Many conservationists would like to see it wiped out here,
regardless of butterflies' fondness for it. Since the box tree
moth is in the process of killing off its invasive namesake
organically, buddleja is the plant that people have decided
to focus on trying to eradicate with the use of poison.

Crop farmers and all those who spray poison are the
enemies of the butterflies and moths that drink buddleja
nectar, including protected species that are not allowed
to be caught and collected under any circumstances. I
understand why some people don't want to continue to
cultivate invasive species. However, I don't understand how
it can be good to deprive these butterflies of a food source
as important as the buddleja, which blooms in mid- and
late summer. I am yet to discover what alternative species
conservationists suggest. Alongside my organic mini war
against the caterpillars on my greens, conservationists'
war against buddleja forms the dark side of what should

be an otherwise easy-going conversation about butterflies. Watching them fly to the buddleja and delight in the nectar of its small, funnel-like flowers is enchanting. I could gaze at them for hours, were some of them not my foes, for butterfly watching truly is something wonderful.

In the spring and early summer, I don't see very many of them at all. I only really spot brimstone butterflies, so yellow that they have earned the German name *Zitronenfalter*, meaning 'lemon moth', although they are certainly not sour to the eye but rather sugar sweet. They are in a hurry when they dance through the garden in April or May. Since my hedge doesn't include alder buckthorn, where the females can lay their eggs, my enthusiasm for them is completely one-sided. I have nothing to offer them so early in the year. That changes in midsummer, when the new generation of brimstones has hatched — they visit the flowers in my garden, in particular the buddleja, where they drink the nectar and rest.

I didn't understand why they only came to the garden in summer until my husband explained what was happening. Freshly hatched brimstones need to build up energy and then look for a place in the hedge to shelter from rain, storms, and birds who don't know how bad these butterflies taste yet. They rest in their hiding places, in a summer slumber that lasts for weeks, until autumn. In October, they awaken and take wing, this time to look for somewhere to overwinter by hanging in the undergrowth, just above ground level. They don't need to find somewhere protected from the frost, as the condensed nectar from the buddleja flowers serves as an antifreeze in their bodies.

If all goes well, I will see the brimstones, which begin their hibernation in late autumn, flying through the garden again in March, April, or maybe even May. At that stage, the brimstones are ten to eleven months old and have a fresh spring look. Observing their life cycle makes me reflective about myself. I think about how badly I need warmth in the winter, and even in those summer months when it is summer in name only. I struggled to get used to the changeable European weather, which varies between hot and cold from one day to the next — I still struggle.

Although the muggy summer heat of my childhood was oppressive, there were no sudden cold snaps that made the days resemble winter in the middle of summer. What am I supposed to do, and how much money am I supposed to spend in order to handle the changeable weather? I have never needed as many coats as I do here. If, as I so often do, I find myself at odds with the inconsistent and unseasonable weather, I think of the brimstone — and am crestfallen. As soon as the clouds reveal the sun, they flutter about, and if a cloud hides the sun, they rest until it comes out again.

I read a lot about these children of the sun, these fluttering butterflies, yet I learnt much more by watching them on the butterfly bush. There they allow me to observe them, often at close quarters, as they eagerly drink nectar. It is a pure pleasure to see a butterfly unrolling its proboscis and feeling its way into the hair's-breadth canal that leads to the nectar. I permit myself to take the time for this indulgence often, watching the butterflies as they open their wings on the buddleja flowers, creating beautiful colours and patterns.

Visitors to the buddleja bush include peacock butterflies, and in some years red admirals and painted ladies. Peacock butterflies come every year but in varying numbers. Sometimes, the flowers are so full that newly arriving butterflies can barely find any space, and their attempts to land cause a reddish-brown whirling chaos. It happens every couple of years. The years when the dappled painted ladies appear in my garden occur at longer intervals; sometimes, it can take a decade until there is another large influx from the south or the south-east. Then, the painted ladies vie for space on the buddleja flowers until barely a single butterfly can land.

The admirals are more regular visitors, albeit in smaller numbers. The broad carmine ring that can be seen when the butterfly sits or is approaching looks like a large, dark, red-rimmed eye, and sometimes even seems to work as one, appearing to blink as the butterfly closes its wings. Again and again, I've seen a sparrow take fright when this 'eye' opened or flew towards it as the bird tried to peck at the butterfly. Sometimes, admirals have even flown towards me, giving the impression of an approaching fist-sized eye.

Peacock butterflies have four eyes: one on each wing. By irregularly but frequently opening and closing their wings, they reveal these eyes, which even have visible light reflexes in the pupils. Closer inspection shows me against whom these eyes are directed. The peacock butterfly not only uses them to fend off birds, but also other insects, primarily bees and large, bee-like hoverflies. Perhaps this defence doesn't work that well against birds out in the open, because they can clearly see that it is a butterfly. However, when a peacock butterfly is resting in a corner or under a roof, where it keeps its wings closed in the upright position, its almost-black underside with fine bark-like markings makes it appear leaf-like. If a bird were to touch this presumed leaf, then the peacock butterfly would open its wings as fast as lightning. Two iridescent pairs of eyes would simultaneously stare out at the hungry bird. The eyespots on the peacock butterfly are unique in that only they reflect UV light, which birds can see. This light reflection really scares birds.

Peacock butterflies drink a lot of nectar from the buddleja flowers in my garden. Of all the species of butterfly that visit this bush, they are generally the ones that stay longest, whereas a brief and quick recharge is typical of a painted lady. The admirals don't allow themselves to linger for long either, as they are en route to the south and have to make use of the favourable migration weather in late summer and autumn. Their destination is the mild-wintered Mediterranean region, while the painted ladies fly to the southern edge of the Sahara in Africa to lay their eggs and develop a winter generation.

Many peacock butterflies also head south, but generally only as far as the northern Mediterranean area, just over the Alps. Some of the summer and autumn generation attempt to overwinter here in Germany — with success if the winter is dry and only moderately cold. It means that in autumn, the peacock butterflies only have a short flight ahead of them; with a favourable wind, they would only need two or three days to travel to the south, over the Alps.

The small tortoiseshell behaves in a similar, but less noticeable, manner. It is also one of the more regular visitors to the buddleja bush, albeit in smaller numbers. Seeing all these butterflies together is one of the summer's most beautiful experiences. I watch them from the patio, from where they are close enough to touch. Despite the unsettled hustle and bustle with which they drink nectar, they create a calming and relaxing atmosphere. It is often abruptly interrupted when, suddenly, an oddity arrives — for example, a swallowtail. When that happens, I am known to jump out of my seat in delight.

This large ochre butterfly has veins on its wings tracing a black lattice pattern, giving it a noble flair. I react with such excitement because it has become so rare. Even upon its arrival, it signals that it will soon vanish again. Its wings do not stop moving as its legs brush against the flowers without fully resting on them. Serenely, it extends its long proboscis and plunges it into a flower for just a fraction of a second. It has to test whether it still contains any nutrition after so many other butterflies were feasting on it before its arrival. Seconds later, it has already gone, evaporating like a mirage. I would sacrifice my carrot tops to its caterpillars because they become such mesmerising beauties. But to date, the swallowtails have only ever visited the buddleja during high summer and have never laid their eggs on my carrot tops in spring. Sadly, they cannot simply be magicked from thin air.

Even more transitory are day-flying moths, whose kin are usually on the wing at dusk and at night. Every summer on the buddleja bush, I see two day-flying moths, both of which bear a striking resemblance to hummingbirds. The most regular is the hummingbird hawk-moth, whose scientific genus name, *Macroglossum stellatarum*, means 'long tongue'. The hummingbird hawk-moth's proboscis is so long that it can drink nectar while hovering, as if standing in the air a few centimetres from the flower. Its wings move so quickly that I can only really sense, not see them, in the blurriness that surrounds its body.

The hummingbird hawk-moth is also a migrant butterfly. In early summer, it flies over the Alps; its descendants return in mid- to late summer. This is certainly an achievement considering their size, which is that of a large bumblebee. Furthermore, these little moths are not shy. Sometimes, I think that they look right at me as they fly from flower to flower. They can be easily confused with another hawk-moth: the broad-bordered bee hawk-moth, which is about the size of a hummingbird hawk-moth but has translucent wings with a dark rim around the outside, so it appears as if only its body is hanging in the air as it hovers beside a flower. I am overjoyed when we discover a broad-bordered bee hawk-moth on the buddleja, because it is so special and so rare (as a visitor to our garden).

Frequently, I spot butterflies that look a little disappointing hovering around the flowers. When I go to take a closer look, they remain brown and ordinary. They are usually very shy, these silver Y moths. They don't belong to the hawk-moth family but to a distantly related family of lepidoptera, the owlet moths. But they are on the wing during the day and eagerly drink nectar for the same reason as the painted ladies, admirals, and hummingbird hawk-moths.

The silver Y moth is also a migratory moth. According to figures, most years it has been the most common migratory moth. Each year millions fly over the Alps in the early summer. I find it deeply touching that the buddleja bush in my garden can serve as a layover, if only a small one, for these moth's and butterflies' intercontinental flights. For that reason, I maintain the buddleja in such a way that it flowers particularly lavishly every year. Its flowers are the butterflies' equivalent to the birds' fat balls, which I also hang on its branches.

I can lose track of my thoughts while watching the comings and goings on the butterfly bush. The origin of the butterflies, the distances they migrate, and how they fit into the larger scales of time and seasons find their way into my thoughts. To know who is drinking the nectar, where the creature comes from, and where it flies to adds to my amazement. Each wing pattern deserves profound contemplation, and each movement of flight is worthy of focus. The only limiting factor is time, which almost always passes by too quickly. And it is a certainty that something particularly exciting will happen at the precise moment I can no longer watch.

Birds in the Garden

... are practically ever-present. They keep checking in on what I am up to. Blackbirds are the most trusting. While none of them are as trusting as Maxi and Emma, other blackbirds, who remain nameless because they kept their distance, still tolerate my presence in the garden far better than other birds. A couple of metres' distance is enough when they search for food in the earth. If a male is singing from the birch or the roof of the small gazebo, he isn't paying any attention to me. Maxi was the only blackbird who made me feel as though he was singing for me when he projected his song from the lower branches.

I like the way that blackbirds behave — they're not as hectic as sparrows, who immediately rush for cover as soon as I set foot on the patio. If I want to watch the sparrows, I have to do so through the living-room window. At the same time, it's the sparrows who benefit most from my presence, since they feed off the fat balls I put out for them the whole year through. I often also provide them with sunflower hearts and wholegrain rice, which I cook, dry, and then scatter on the patio. I actually put it out for the collared doves, but they are often too slow. By the time they notice there is something for them, the sparrows have already pecked almost all of it away.

Blackbirds sometimes eat sunflower hearts, particularly in extremely dry springs, like that of 2020. Worms were not rising from the earth and there were no insect larvae on the bone-dry soil. Out of necessity, they ate the sunflower hearts, which are almost too hard for them to digest. Nevertheless, they survived; I don't know whether this was thanks to our feeding, but a pair of blackbirds did stay in our garden and attempted to nest.

After the start of May, when it had rained again and the bushes were thick and green, the female built three nests. She built her first nest in a niche in the garden fence. She clearly only noticed that the neighbourhood cats often walk along that fence after she had completed her build.

Her next two attempts, one in a nesting cove for black redstarts under the garage roof and another in the thuja hedge, failed because magpies noticed her nest building and stole the eggs. The empty eggshells lay on the patio.

Even so, the male still sang at full volume in the mornings and evenings, and often during the day, as if he were boasting that he had the best blackbird territory of all. The female still had two months in which to try again. Last year, we were sure that the pair managed to raise a brood successfully in the end. Some juvenile blackbirds, with their easily recognisable speckled breast plumage, spent months in the garden searching for food, always in close proximity to their parents. They appeared healthy and perky. This year, our blackbirds once again managed to nurture a fledgling, maybe even two.

When I watch the blackbirds, I pity their generally unsuccessful attempts to breed, despite their sheer tirelessness. It's hard to believe that they are better off in the garden than out in the forests, but maybe that is because I see so much of their lives in the garden. Even long walks in the woods do not really offer an insight into the lives of the birds whose songs fill me with such joy. In the garden, the birds are close to me both spatially and emotionally, even when they remain needlessly shy, like the sparrows. I only need to open the door to the patio for a whole group of them to shoot away as if I were a sparrowhawk.

In contrast, the blackbirds and the collared doves wait to see where I will go. They keep their distance but don't break into a panic when I appear. Are sparrows' brains so incapable of learning? I ponder this question all the more because the sparrows are the first to return when I hang out a new fat ball. It means that they watched me put out food for them from a distance that they considered safe, for example from the top of a tree crown.

Although they keep their distance from me, they quickly accepted my dog. Occasionally, the birds hopped so close to him that I thought they would start pulling hairs from his coat as he lay on the patio and gazed almost trance-like at the garden. His undercoat was highly coveted. They came closer to me when I laid his hair out on the patio after grooming him than when I hung out the food. The bravest ones, generally the males, hurried over in elegant flight, grabbed a clump of hair, and flew with it to the roof of the gazebo. There they would readjust it in their beaks so that they could continue back to their nests under the roofs of the houses in the neighbourhood. Some of the bundles of fur they grabbed were so big that I wouldn't have thought the sparrows would be able to see where they were going.[1]

Some mornings, when empty nets hung on the branches because the fat balls had been pecked away,

---

1 Recent studies have found that if a dog has been given a spot-on treatment against fleas or ticks, then its fur could kill the sensitive chicks in the nest. My dog's fur was not toxic because it had not been poisoned!

sparrows would come up to the patio and conspicuously hop about. I got the impression that they wanted to attract my attention, knowing that the shut glass doors offered them the same protection as the windows through which I watched their acrobatic antics on the fat balls. If I opened the doors, they would scatter and vanish in a fraction of a second, even though it was they who had wanted to catch my attention and alert me that their food was gone in the first place. It was also a waste of energy. Needless to say, minutes later, they were doing gymnastics on the newly hung fat balls as if they had received an ordered delivery. Well, in a way they *had* ordered it, and I had reacted like an obedient servant. The nature of sparrows is simply different to that of blackbirds. And even the two kinds of sparrows do not behave in an entirely similar way.

Although house sparrows, generally in a flock of approximately fifteen, are the most common visitors, several tree sparrows also feed from the fat balls. They are a little smaller than the house sparrows, but it is the rounder, darker patch on their white cheeks that reveals their identity. The males and females look alike, both of them having a brown cap. Despite the few differences in appearance, their behaviour seemed to be very sparrow-like to me. At least, until I studied them in more detail and noticed a difference that I found remarkable: how tree sparrows deal with fat balls.

Tree sparrows fly directly at them, land on them almost as elegantly as titmice, and peck out the bits they like.

House sparrows attempt to reach the food from a short distance, while perched on a branch. It looks clumsy — and it is, too. They stretch their necks as far as possible in order to reach a fat ball. Only then do they dare attempt the gymnastic challenge of hanging on to it. Their dexterity gives the tree sparrows a major advantage. Usually, they have to make way for the more dominant house sparrows; a house sparrow only needs to issue a brief threat with its slightly opened beak in order to keep the tree sparrows away. Nevertheless, the few tree sparrows who regularly visit the fat balls manage to feed their young.

Their offspring come with them and sit on a branch right next to the fat ball, despite being surrounded by house sparrows of both sexes. They sit on the most level twig they can find and beg incessantly by quivering their wings. House sparrow juveniles behave in the same way. I laugh at how the young, positioned right beside the fat ball, take it for granted that their parents will feed them and don't make any attempt to help themselves to the food that is literally hanging in front of their beaks. The yellow edge on their beaks reveals them to be fully fledged juvenile birds. Children, I think involuntarily. And their poor parents doing all the work. Instead of eating themselves, the house and tree sparrows feed their offspring just because they are begging. Parents are indulgent.

Close by, just a few branches along, an elegant male house sparrow with a large black bib, wings hanging down and tail pointing up at an angle, is chirping in front of a female who is feigning disinterest. The young have flown the nest so a new brood can follow. That means these sparrows are courting, which is a joy to watch. Suddenly, a nearby sparrow starts to panic and flees like a miniature rocket into the bushes. All the others follow, irrespective of whether they were courting or busy on the fat ball. Sparrow life. I enjoy it, even though it is completely hectic.

It seems even more so when compared to the collared doves, who appear calm, roaming around under the fat ball in search of any fallen bits. Their plumage shimmers sandy brown with a light-pink tone, their steps are deliberate, and head bobbing accompanies every movement. The thin black bar on the back of their neck is revealed with every bob. A certain grace comes to mind when characterising their appearance. They embody calm itself when compared to the nervousness of the sparrows.

As birds, sparrows and collared doves are so different that they don't seem as though they would be compatible. Both of them live exclusively in villages and small towns, always in the vicinity of humans, and both originate from the Near East. However, house sparrows aligned themselves with humans thousands of years ago. They followed crop farmers as they spread west. Issa Kobayashi wrote in one of his famous haikus, 'Young sparrows get out of the way! A great horse is coming!'

It was much later, only about a hundred years ago, that collared doves had the 'idea' of entering into the world of humans. They succeeded, so much so that their mating call, a very monotonous 'coo-cooo-cuck', annoys people all year round — they are always in the mood for courting. From late summer to spring, the house sparrows behave significantly more calmly, although they still flock together, almost as though they want to advertise that they are (still) here.

I have two species of titmice in my garden: the great tit with a black stroke running down its yellow belly, and the smaller blue tit with its light-blue cap. They are always quiet; they even go without singing noticeably loud songs during their breeding season. I often only become aware of them when I'm watching the comings and goings on the fat balls. They approach, land somewhere on the ball, and peck out what they like.

Clearly, the presence of sparrows doesn't bother the titmice. If several sparrows cluster around a fat ball at the same time, the titmice wait until one finds it too difficult to keep clinging to the ball and flies away. Then one of the titmice will vault over with such fabulous ease that you would believe it was doing a demonstration to teach the clumsier birds its elegant gymnastic tricks. I am constantly impressed by their quirks and differences because they show the variety of birds in the garden, who live together but at the same time have independent lives dictated by their differing natures.

Evidently, legs are a limiting factor for these birds. It is especially noticeable when starlings come and try to peck something from the fat balls. They land on the closest possible branch with visible effort and, since they are considerably larger than the sparrows, they can just about reach the hanging ball with their long-pointed beaks. However, touching it is not enough; they also need to be able to peck at it. The first contact with their beaks makes the ball move, and subsequent contact causes it to sway like a pendulum being repeatedly pushed with every touch. My mood also swings ... between amusement and sympathy.

Despite their best efforts, the starlings barely manage to get even the tiniest piece of fat. The fat ball eludes them, then it swings back at them without the starlings getting a proper chance to peck at it. Visibly frustrated, they fly to the ground and search for any crumbs that might have fallen during the sparrows' feast. They pace around in a ludicrous manner, striding step by step with an erect body. A starling is too slow to compete for crumbs if a blackbird is also searching for them there. A blackbird can hop over to the food and, with its measured steps, will reach it before a starling can. However, the blackbirds don't even attempt to get to the sought-after fat balls hanging in the bushes. Their feet, with which they can hop so elegantly, are no good for acrobatics in the branches.

I note the different ways the garden birds move when I watch them feeding. Although blackbirds can also run quickly, they generally hop like sparrows and move less noticeably than finches. In contrast, starlings pace, collared doves scuttle, and titmice barely set foot on the ground — the titmice's domain is up in the branches; they are acrobats and only rarely pedestrians.

Once I had made myself aware of the differences between all the birds in the garden, I understood why starlings always appear immediately after we have mown the lawn. They step rather daintily over the freshly revealed ground. Here and there, suddenly poking their beaks a couple of centimetres into the soil, twisting it a little, and pulling something up: a worm or the larvae of an insect. Blackbirds also hop on freshly mowed spots and exhaustively examine them. Collared doves are not as interested, probably because they wouldn't find any seeds on the freshly cut lawn. The sparrows hop about on it in search of insects.

For a few days after the grass has been mown, the lawn is teeming with birds — until the grass regrows and the allure for the birds has vanished. The hopping blackbirds scour the mowed areas for longer than the striding starlings. Sparrows are the first to return to their usual behaviour, unless they were in the process of collecting new nest material. A couple of days after mowing, they will find that the freshly dried and still flexible blades of grass have turned to straw, particularly good for nest building. However, my garden doesn't provide them with what they really want:

open sandy areas where they can take dust baths. I do have several birdbaths, though, which all the birds in my garden use, splashing drops of water about.

Sadly, the blackcaps are completely uninterested in the mowed grass. I hoped to be finally able to gaze at them extensively at leisure, out in the open, but they did not emerge from the cover of the hedge. Not even the beautifully voiced male with his black crown, whose warbling could be heard until early summer. At first, he could be heard singing several times during the day. From May, his performances were relegated primarily to the evenings and early mornings, but he reverted back to singing throughout the daytime again in June. This pattern led me to believe that he had attracted a female and was nesting. Sadly, I never saw any young blackcaps. Maybe the brood had fallen victim to a cat. Magpies and crows would probably not have ventured through such dense thicket. Or maybe the chicks kept themselves well hidden, which was my favourite theory.

In addition to the birds that have claimed the garden as either a part of or the centre of their territory, other birds occasionally visit. A lesser whitethroat sings each year between mid-April and the start of May, but he doesn't stay — most likely because no females put in an appearance. The nesting cove, where blackbirds once tried to build a nest, has yet to be of interest to any black redstarts, which we would love to attract to the garden. A smoky-black male sang from the neighbour's roof so regularly and intensively that the house must have formed the centre of its territory.

Greenfinches were regular visitors to our garden for many years. The males trilled their song and performed vacillating air stunts, reminiscent of unbalanced paper planes. A couple of years ago, they were hit by an epidemic that decimated greenfinch populations.

Why no chaffinches feel at home in the garden is a mystery to me. At least one of them could be heard singing from the end of February into the summer but, frustratingly, it remained in the neighbour's garden and didn't regularly pop over to mine in search of food. Maybe we didn't mow the grass enough — finches do not like long grass. A visit from a wryneck in April 2020 was surely only down to his need for a brief rest during his journey to a suitable breeding area. He didn't even have the time to make his rapid 'quee, quee, quee' call.

I had to get used to the fact that magpies checked our garden each day. Not because I don't think they're pretty; with their black and white feathers, they really are something special. The long tail feathers of their plumage shimmer a particularly beautiful metallic green and violet. Nobody needed to explain to me that magpies are very intelligent. They quickly realised that I didn't welcome them on account of their attempts to take down the fat ball and fly away with it. Seeing me working in the kitchen was enough to convince them immediately to fly off.

Nevertheless, they have repeatedly managed to steal whole fat balls, as I can't permanently guard the garden.

I have to accept that when they steal eggs, and most likely also small chicks, from blackbird nests, it is a natural process. This poaching is certainly more natural than the hunting done by neighbourhood cats because the cats have more than enough food at home. They don't need to provide for themselves and their kittens in the way that magpies do, yet the cats continue to hunt.

A magpie's biggest enemy is a carrion crow, but hawks and other birds of prey also stalk them. No species is ever completely safe. After seeing a sparrowhawk chasing the sparrows in our garden several times, I came to understand better why the smaller birds react so violently to every movement, even when it is just me, their benefactor, going out into the garden. It's not possible to look first and fly away later. To survive they must do it the other way around.

Occasionally, certain feathered friends that I class as optical treats stop by the garden, for instance goldfinches with their red faces and the yellow markings on their wings. In addition to their understated beauty, I also find their gentle 'whit-a-whit, whit' call particularly charming. However, even more delightful are the waxwings, which put in an appearance in some winters. Their calls sound silvery, their feathers appear silky, and since they show little timidity around humans, I can watch them at arm's length through binoculars as they eat privet and dogwood berries, which no other bird likes. They repeatedly raise their crests and trill. If they eat mistletoe berries, they often drag seeds behind them, attached to long sticky threads, until they land somewhere. The seeds then remain there and may grow into a mistletoe bush.

The list of birds that I get to see in the garden would be really long were I to write it down. It wouldn't signify very much, because the majority of the birds I've seen only land briefly or simply fly over; the garden and my work in it mean very little to them. Rarities may be charming, but my connection to them lacks the magic of my connection to the garden's regulars. The blackbird who watches me turn the beds, and then searches the fresh earth or scrabbles around in a flowerpot, holds a different significance for me. It gives me the feeling that I belong to it and am part of its life.

Earwigs

Some creatures and plants are useful. Unfortunately, usefulness does not necessarily guarantee beauty; rather, the opposite is usually the case. Earwigs constitute a prime example. There are certainly many more beautiful insects with nicer names — ladybirds, for instance.

Earwigs have no luck with their names in either English or German, in which they are known as *Ohrwürmer* or *Ohrwusseler*, roughly translating to 'ear worms' or 'ear scuttlers'. That last name might sound strange, but it suits this type of insect far better than its other names because you tend to find earwigs scuttling about where you least expect them. They are not worms, and even the prefix 'ear' is misleading for it refers to their ear- or heart-shaped pincers as opposed to the myth that earwigs crawl into people's ears as they sleep.

They can use these pincers to pinch, but their nip is harmless and an acceptable price to pay for their other services. Anyone, like myself, who has tried to do the earwig's work with their own fair hands knows why I hold these creatures in particularly high esteem and treat them exceptionally well should one stray into the house. That said, I do return them to the garden, as in the house they are unable to fulfil the biological purpose I so admire: combatting aphids.

But, first things first. Every gardening book teaches that earwigs are useful, but reality is often very different and much more complex than they describe. My song of praise for the earwig starts with a long and exceptionally unpleasant prelude. The roses are blooming, which, of course, fills me with joy. The hibiscus bush is turning green, which would also make me happy if it were not for the blue-grey to black patches of aphids forming where buds have started to develop. Patches that, at first, irritate me, then make me angry, and ultimately force me to carry out desperate acts ... with nettle manure.

The stink of it greets me as soon as I open the door to the garden. That I can tolerate; however, as soon as I begin to use it to fight off the aphids, I also start to stink of it. I hope the concentration is right — strong enough to kill the aphids but not so strong that it burns the hibiscus shoots that are bearing buds. I managed to squash the first colonies with my fingers on my own, wearing rubber gloves for protection. However, Marigold gloves were developed for use in the kitchen, not for aphid warfare, and the juices of squashed aphids permeated the gloves and became unpleasantly noticeable on my skin. In modern parlance, you could say these fluids are 'sustainable'.

My husband forwent rubber gloves and had to use hard soap to attempt to wash off the aphid pulp that had sunk into the outer layer of his skin, with moderate success and sympathetic patience on my part. Nevertheless, he quickly gave up. Unfortunately. That forced me to start producing liquid manure from nettles.

After spreading it around my hibiscus bushes, they smelt typical of the countryside, where slurry floods have become commonplace. The bushes most likely wished for rain as much as I did. Not immediately, but at the right time: hopefully an overnight, continuous rain. Although a storm shower would have a cleansing effect, it would also benefit the aphids that survived my nettle treatment. Constant rain also hinders the formation of flowers. Somewhere in between is the ideal rain, which, of course, fails to make an appearance when required. And so, I need my friends, the earwigs.

I treasure them so much: I don't jump back in fright if one of them falls from the rose that I have pulled towards me to smell its fine fragrance. I do not scream when one crawls up my trouser leg while I am eating breakfast on the patio. Although I am intolerant when midges and horseflies approach, I patiently suffer the admittedly unpleasant crawling of the earwigs. I remind myself of what I must look like to them, dressed like an astronaut in a much too big and unflattering plastic jacket, spending hours in the garden waging war on the aphids.

These pests bear my attempts at destruction with a calmness that I only understood when I realised what their lives consist of: drink and give birth, give birth and drink, without end. Reproduction requires no mate, so a newborn aphid can begin this cycle immediately, before it has even had its first taste of hibiscus sap. It is a great gift from nature that earwigs eat these breeders and their sucking spawn.

Earwigs are just like presents; you don't normally get a lot of them at once, except on special occasions. I feel the earwigs' absence precisely when the fight against the aphids is reaching its high point. To add insult to injury, during this phase of radical combat, which damages my sense of smell for days and leaves brown marks on my fingers, I mainly only encounter earwigs when washing lettuce freshly brought in from the garden. They flounder in the water and wave their pincers as I try to fish them out, often trying to escape my rescue attempts. They are barely in my hand for a second before they run back into the water.

When I finally manage to catch them, I loosely cover them with my other hand and carry them into the garden and to the hibiscus bushes like a treasure. That is where they should have been, not on the lettuce. They should also stop all the somersaulting and jumping they are doing in an attempt to flee. Although these acrobatics are amusing, I don't want them to be doing it, because if they escape, the journey to the aphid colony will be much too far for them to travel without my help. Why don't these nifty little insects understand that I am going to such efforts to protect and help them?

Such contemplations make my mood swing between distrust and discontentment. I read in one of Dave Goulson's books that 'aphids are the perfect bite-sized snacks' for earwigs. However, this begs the urgent question: do they know that? And why have their comrades-in-arms, the green lacewings and ladybirds, also not realised that my garden has the finest aphids?

I once found earwigs in the remains of some green tea that I had left overnight on the patio and was planning to use as a particularly organic fertiliser to distribute among the neediest of my plants the next day. They scurried out of the clumps of leaves. I had not expected there to be earwigs in the tea. They should have been out working, battling aphids.

Despite all conceivable protective measures, which should have benefitted them, earwigs have not saved me from having to brew my nettle concoction. Every year, the low effectiveness of trying to combat aphids biologically using earwigs, lacewings, and the like drives me towards chemicals. For I have to admit, my nettle manure is a means of chemical combat. At least it hasn't been bought and synthesised by a company, but rather is produced by me.

My song of praise for earwigs generally has a bitter aftertaste, or rather after-smell. The kind of spring weather that stops aphids from reproducing en masse is extremely rare. It is only when such weather arrives that my earwigs and ladybirds manage to keep aphid numbers below the damage threshold. This success is mainly thanks to Asian ladybirds; with their support, earwigs can cope with the number of aphids. Had they not arrived, it might be their European cousins, the two-spot and seven-spot ladybirds, doing the job. Or maybe they never would have been able to keep aphid numbers down as effectively.

Obviously, much is assumed but very little is exhaustively studied. Had our two-spot and seven-spot ladybirds been effective enough as aphid eaters, we would not have had to enlist the help of the East Asian ladybirds. But even with their help, all the ladybirds, earwigs, and green lacewings in my garden cannot keep the aphids at bay. As I said before, it is the reason the argument that Asian ladybirds are pushing out European ladybirds does not convince me.

Pests and Weeds

It all began with itchy spots. They were smaller than mosquito bites, deep red, and didn't develop into raised bumps like mosquito bites do. I had them in places I could guarantee no mosquito could have accessed, and so I suspected my dog. Like all dogs, he would occasionally scratch, whether he had fleas or not. Maybe a flea jumped off him, I thought as I treated the itchy spots with a few drops of Swedish bitters, my special tincture against insect bites. Although it eased the itching, it helped much less than it normally did against mosquito bites or horsefly stings.

In answer to my question, 'Have you given me a flea?' the dog reacted as he usually would when asked an unfounded or even a well-founded question — with a wag of his tail and a particularly loyal, hangdog look. The red spots were increasing in number, and the new ones itched more than the old ones. Even after a deep treatment, allowing disinfecting alcohol to sink into my skin for minutes, the itch could not be notably suppressed.

I got bites on my legs from my ankle upwards, as well as further up my body. I was even more perplexed when my dog began biting between his toes more and more often. He could deal with ticks: he would sometimes be able to show us where one had attached itself and allow us to remove it. Then he would sniff the spot in order to assure himself that we really had found the tick, which was practically fit to burst with his blood.

Sometimes, he would bite at them with visible pleasure. In doing so, he spared me from having to squash the blighter with a flat stone that I had laid out. I used this method to kill ticks that I discovered in his fur before they latched on and sucked his blood, as I couldn't manage it with my fingernails alone. My dog knew the procedure. I only had to say the word 'tick', and he would stand stock-still and let his fur be searched to have the ticks removed.

He willingly gave me his paw so I could search his toes for ticks, but he didn't move in the way he usually did when stretching his soft paw towards me. This time, I got the feeling that he had to force himself. He watched, full of expectation, but couldn't stop himself from frequently jerking his leg away. I found nothing. I had barely let go of his paw when he lay down and started to bite it again, using a canine and curling his lips right up. My red spots were also itching again. I was suffering with him. I tried to control myself and not scratch.

It turned out that midsummer heat was not particularly helpful in this regard. A lukewarm shower brought me some relief. I sprayed my dog's paws, so they were wet, upon which he started to dig a hole somewhere in the garden and returned with dirty paws that required immediate washing. In short: we were both really suffering.

Although dusk brought cooler temperatures, the night remained Mediterranean after the thirty-five-degree heat that we had endured for much of the day. We were still itching. There were no mosquitoes; it was too hot and dry for them. If fleas were the culprits, there would have to be a lot of them, at least a dozen. They weren't responsible. The pest lurked in the garden: everywhere and invisible, at least to my eyes.

I, and most likely the dog, had been afflicted by harvest mites. The teeny-tiny beasts burrowed into the skin, where it is thin and soft. For the dog, that was between his toes and a few places on his sides, and for me it was almost everywhere. Bloodsuckers dream of delicate human skin, almost as if it were made for them. Waterborne larvae and worms dig into skin almost effortlessly, while on land, ticks, fleas, and bugs do the dirty work. Horseflies of all sizes successfully attack from the air and, of course, there are mosquitoes, mosquitoes, mosquitoes ... That mites were also among their ranks hit me particularly hard, because I had them in my own garden, could not see them, and could not avoid them.

These harvest mites are part of the *Trombiculidae* family, and they are found primarily in grasslands that were once grazed by sheep in the period from midsummer to early autumn, particularly at the time when the tomatoes ripen. This means that decades ago, on the spot where my garden stands, there will have been a low-nutrient meadow. Sheep would have grazed on it in the autumn. A flock is still in residence nearby, kept here to graze and conserve the landscape. If we came close to them while walking our dog, the sheepdogs protecting them would bark loudly at us. We understood that we should choose a better route to walk and sought it out.

Letting sheep graze on a field in order to conserve the landscape is a good thing. It is far better than maintaining it mechanically using mowers, which cut everything short and small, including blindworms, lizards, toads, and mice. The shredded caterpillars and chrysalises of protected butterflies, some of the many victims of this type of maintenance, go unnoticed. They are only missed later, when the butterflies that should be on the wing do not appear.

I thought it was plausible that these harvest mites were a relic from the days when sheep grazed the land that was now my garden. On the other hand, I thought it was less plausible that they had remained there for decades without any sheep. One day, I felt a small, barely noticeable tickle on my lower arm. A tick was creeping along up towards my T-shirt with a speed that I had not thought possible for the flat, misshapen thing. Since I had just been working in the bushes in front of the fence, it must have come from there. Oh no, not that as well! As if harvest mites weren't bad enough. I had protected myself against them, apparently quite successfully, with repellents that I carefully sprayed or rubbed on my ankles and calves, depending on which one I was using. I like the spray containing cedar oil best, because it doesn't smell as pungent, and I don't have an allergic reaction to it. After discovering the tick, I also tried to protect my arms adequately.

What is the difference between my garden and the alluvial forests full of mosquitoes and horseflies, or the woods with their ticks and masses of midges? My garden should be a mini paradise: full of sparrows and other nice birds, butterflies, wild bees, ladybirds, and wildflowers. With soft moss, upon which I like to walk barefoot early in the morning to refresh myself for the start of the day. Would I still be able to do this if tiny mites were lurking in the grass? Instead of walking barefoot, would I have to wear fastened-up shoes or garden sandals with raised heels in the mornings and evenings, the most beautiful times in the garden?

I was eternally grateful that harvest mites don't transmit any diseases. Had they not been in my garden, I would have been content not to know of their existence. Unlike ticks, they are clearly not ubiquitous and can only be found in those areas where sheep once grazed or still do. They cannot starve themselves and hold out for decades; they need carriers. It's enough for such a grazing area to exist in the near vicinity, as there are plenty of animals that carry and spread them.

Harvest mites are similar to the ticks sucking my dog's blood. If one of them escapes my notice and falls into the garden, then we are in for trouble. She will have undoubtedly mated with a male just beforehand, and will now be able to lay her hundreds of eggs in the garden. Hundreds of tick children, cutely named 'nymphs' by zoologists, will hatch from the eggs, latch on to mice, and continue to develop, despite many of them dying, until they grow to a size that allows them to drink the blood of dogs, cats, and even humans — and continue to reproduce.

The harvest mites in the garden will have been brought here in a similar manner. It could have been cats that were afflicted, since sheep no longer live in this built-up and settled area. Maybe the summer had just been too good; after all, harvest mites prefer dry, warm, and thinly covered grassy areas. Maybe I could get rid of the mites if my dog kept the cats out of my garden — a shimmer of hope began to grow. However, our brains are excellently capable of latching on to shimmers of hope, in a similar fashion to how they quickly think up excuses after a mishap.

The first time I was confronted with harvest mites was in Munich, shortly after my arrival from Japan. Back then, the itching was so bad I feared that I had caught shingles. The doctor gave me an injection, which helped, and he explained about harvest mites. They are common on the outskirts of Munich and rife in some places, like sheep farms. The second massive attack hit me in the beautiful old garden of a small castle in Burgundy. They even targeted my husband, who usually suffers much less from them, owing to the exposure to the stings and bites of various bloodsuckers he has had since his childhood, which has allowed him to develop a certain immunity to them.

We were nearly driven to distraction: the first harvest mite assault had been on a farm, the next in the grounds of a castle in Burgundy, and now they were in my garden — my dog surely regarded this as his garden, too. We took him to the vet because he had begun licking his wounds. He also received an injection and medication, both of which helped.

When hanging out the washing in the garden, I wore wellies. When doing things like tending the roses, I was surrounded by the scent of cedar oil: it became the fragrance that encapsulated that harvest-mite-ridden summer. As the weeks went by and the weather stayed dry, the mites became rarer; this trend has continued over the years. Is it wishful thinking to hope that the summers will continue to remain dry, as summer storms never follow the same pattern? It must be possible to starve and eradicate them somehow, like what happens to slugs, for whom a dry summer is a catastrophe, while for us, who want to be rid of them, it is literally a gift from the heavens.

A glance to the sky abruptly interrupts this train of thought. A word suddenly comes to mind that summarises everything that prevents my garden, my haven, from being or becoming a complete paradise. Pests. I have no choice other than to accept that in my garden there are and will continue to be pests. You cannot create a truly worry-free paradise, no matter how hard you work and strive for it. The challenge is to embrace it as it is and how it develops. An unsettling but also reassuring conclusion, as it acknowledges that what happens in the garden isn't (just) down to me — what happens, happens. The garden, every garden, has its own life and past history. Nothing is completely new, not even the perfectly prepared beds.

Gardening means planting, selecting, nurturing, and weeding. It can be elegantly described as designing. Part of this process is deciding what is a plant and what is a weed. For me, this distinction does not exist clearly. Rather, I regard it as something akin to an East Asian yin and yang relationship; the two separate sections, despite starting from opposite poles, merge into each other. This stance blurs the distinction between plant and weed.

I have learnt that people in Germany describe this with the phrase 'opposites attract'. It is very true: everything that I do to benefit the lettuce, tomatoes, cucumbers, potatoes, or even flowers also, and inevitably unwittingly, encourages the growth of other, unintended plants and animals. Weeds move in with the plants. Books tell me that all gardening becomes defensive combat, and that garden chores are always about fighting against something. These are facts that are seemingly so self-evident that they are accepted as how things should and always will be. They offer a great excuse to complain: be it about wildly growing weeds or snails that the heavens have favoured with ideal weather.

I try to resist complaining even though I am close to desperation in my battle against aphids. Instead, I observe how the creatures live and how the weeds thrive. It's educational — it helps to create more understanding. In other words, when I look more closely at the weeds, I discover more about all nature, rather than just about what I would like to harvest. In doing so, I hope that, in line with the ju-jitsu principles of my samurai ancestors, I, at least sometimes, recognise my weaknesses and allow myself to make peace with my adversaries. Softness against coarseness. To garden without poison and where possible without blades, instead applying gentle direction. Of course, I repeatedly fail, but failure is part of the process. Cutting back is not the same as extermination. Where there is an opportunity for more gentle gardening, I favour it, for instance limiting the growth of the nettles.

Somehow nettles always manage to get their seeds into the well-fertilised soil of my garden and grow. The signature itchiness on my skin occasionally reveals that nettles are forming, earlier than a critical glance around the garden could. Over the years, I have also learnt that all the caterpillars of the various butterflies that live in my garden working in tandem can't prevent nettles from running riot, no matter how much effort I put into growing nectar-rich flowers for the peacock butterfly and the small tortoiseshell (both of whose caterpillars love to eat nettles) to find throughout the summer. I even invite the mother-of-pearl moth, named after its mother-of-pearl wings, to make itself at home on my most delicious nettle patch — its caterpillars eat and live inside rolled-up nettle leaves. The invitation is also extended to some other species of butterfly, but they can clearly find enough nettles for their caterpillars in better locations than my garden. They fail as organic helpers in curbing nettle growth — unfortunately.

It doesn't surprise me. During my walks in the alluvial woods or out in the forests, I notice that no other weed is as common or thrives as rampantly as the nettle. I can't really describe it as a weed, as there was a time when it was very common to eat nettles in a salad or to cut them into small pieces to feed to the chickens and young geese in the garden. Once the stinging hairs have been rendered harmless, a foraged nettle salad can be very healthy. I have not acquired a taste for this type of natural food — I have a different use for nettles. I cut them up and soak them in water to make an 'infusion' to combat the aphids on the shrubs, in particular the hibiscus bushes. For this concoction, I need more nettle shoots than my garden can even come close to providing. I get what I need from the alluvial forest.

When cutting nettles out there, I get some surprised looks. Maybe from people who know the old farming ways and think I have ducklings to feed. Or maybe they think that I am some kind of natural healer. Nettles are famous for their diuretic and blood-purifying effects. They can be found in non-dispensing pharmacies, but in contrast to nettles found in nature, these products are not free, even though they are definitely no better than if they were freshly prepared. Due to their usefulness, I get along with nettles very well.

My relationship with dandelions is more difficult, especially now that my neighbours no longer keep rabbits and don't need my first-class organic dandelion leaves anymore. Dandelions are now growing in every possible gap between the paving slabs in my garden, even at the entrance to the house, and they are joined by a few other plants, too.

The prevailing point of view is that this kind of wild growth doesn't make a good impression. On the other hand, poisoned gaps between paving stones do apparently make a good impression. Leaving moss to grow on the fence and allowing dandelions to burst from between the cracks has consequences. Children, spurred on by over-eager teachers, stuck a note alluding to the problem on the garden fence facing the street. It was signed by 'the environment detectives'. The suspension of school caused by the COVID-19 pandemic has hopefully stopped such strange environmental education for a while … a small positive effect.

The focus of the young environment detectives is not surprising when the streets in my local area provide a large-scale demonstration of how clean everything must be — flowers on the verges even need a special permit (a sign saying: 'here is a flower meadow'). In order to remain at least in the vicinity of what the local area deems 'tidy', I have to pull and dig plants out from between the cracks. I can't help but admire their capacity for persistent growth, even under the most hostile conditions. Anyway, how it looks inside my garden should be my business alone. It would never have occurred to me to present my garden to the public fully gravelled and without plant life, or with perfect, artificially inserted conifers, until I saw some gardens that actually looked like that — and was shocked. They might be easy to maintain but come at the cost of being hostile to life. Artificial grass suits them; poison is not necessary where there is nothing left to kill.

It is not worth arguing about taste. Not even about my own, I add mentally. Anyway, my husband thinks that I have a tendency to change my mind too much and make things too different. Although, he assures me that he doesn't mean that the garden should simply grow and become a wilderness, as that would cause it to lose its charm and species diversity.

From time to time, when I have a spare moment to observe them, I remember the rare species that we have. One plant that is always a source of fascination goes by the name of compass plant, or prickly lettuce. It primarily grows in the gaps between the wall of the house and the flagstone path on the south and south-east sides, which benefit from a lot of direct sun. The name 'compass' is rather accurate; when possible, its serrated leaves point to the north and south. As a result, the midday sun doesn't hit it too hard, something I can tell from the unique shadow it casts at this time of day. In the early morning, its shadow is broad. As the day goes on, it gets increasingly narrow until, when the sun is at its height, it becomes extremely thin. Then it grows broader again in the afternoon. Only when something else shades it from the direct midday sun does the compass plant deviate from its compass alignment. But why does the compass plant behave this way while other plants in the garden do not?

On investigating this question, I discovered something very unexpected: the Mediterranean compass plant is an ancestor of the lettuce, the common green salad head, to be precise. I have to protect the ones that I grow against the midday sun, otherwise they drink more water than

I can pour over them, and they won't grow in standing water or mud. At first glance, the compass plant and the lettuce do not have much in common. If I pull a leaf from the compass plant, a drop of 'milk' leaks out, just as with large lettuce leaves. However, compass plant leaves are hard and have serrated edges and rows of downward-pointing prickles on their veins. I would not like to put them in my mouth. The slugs clearly have the same opinion, for they either completely avoid the compass plants or perform perplexingly adventurous climbs up them, leaving traces of slime behind for me to follow.

A couple of years ago, when a site marked for construction on the edge of town had a large population of compass plants, the effect of their rows of prickles was evident. Even though the plot was teeming with so many large brown slugs that even my dog had difficulty not treading on them during his morning walk, there was almost no evidence of nibbling on the compass plants. In contrast, in the damp early summer, the slugs demolished my lettuces to such an extent that it drove me to despair. It appeared that only a handful of them were needed to do this to my garden, yet there were thousands of them at the compass plant site and the leaves remained uneaten.

Human intervention has caused the rows of prickles to disappear and the leaf surfaces to become bigger and bigger, and because of that the lettuce has become more tender and desirable for the slugs. The compass plant serves as a guide in more than just the geographical sense — in a historical one, too. I let it grow and flower against the house wall, its yellow flowers reminding me of miniature dandelions. It is actually a close botanical relative of the dandelion, which leads me to believe that their leaves must have a similar make-up. This fact makes me ponder: no matter how different they appear upon superficial examination, plants in the garden generally aren't that different from each other. Many of them are relatives — and they all attract the not-so-desirable creatures that come into the garden. Weeds and pests are corresponding yin and yang poles; many things connect them.

Little flowers, which I love for their delicate subtlety, demonstrate this point beautifully. Also because they quickly wither as growth is really gathering momentum in April. The smallest flowers growing in my garden, common whitlow-grass and hairy bittercress, are so small that I would miss them were I not looking for them. Both of them are *Cruciferae*: they have four petals positioned opposite each other and are related to cress. I like growing cress to season various dishes or crown a salad with its delicate but bitter taste. Their flowers are small; the ones on the common whitlow-grass are downright tiny. What sticks out to me when I notice them in the garden in April is that the small rosettes that their leaves form sit directly on the surface of the soil. Of course, that is only possible when the soil is essentially free of all other vegetation.

The leaves of the common whitlow-grass are elongated and somewhat jagged, while the hairy bittercress leaves are roundish. If pods with seeds develop, the ones on the hairy bittercress are long and thin, while on the common whitlow-grass they are shorter and rounder. Although these subtleties represent the beauty in detail, they are not the main reason for my admiration, which stems from their ability to grow from almost nothing. They grow and thrive in the most inhospitable places; all they need is some soil and light, which makes me think they characterise the very modest end of the spectrum of wild plants in my garden. Rapidly multiplying dandelions and nettles are found on the other end of the spectrum. These small plants show me how few places exist that are actually poor in nutrients. I look out for their flowers in April as a reminder not to fertilise the garden too much. It gets many nutrients, in particular nitrogen compounds, via the air anyway. We can smell these compounds in 'good country air' as they are emitted from manure gases. They are one of the many external influences that have an effect on the garden.

Another external influence comes from combustion engines, which are a source of fertilising nitrogen compounds. Each year, these engines release thirty kilograms of nitrogen per hectare into the air (calculated as pure nitrogen, not according to the various weights of the nitrogen compounds). It is no surprise then that even unfertilised grass grows far too fast and needs to be mowed whether you want to or not. Although I like to let these small plants live, in particular the common whitlow-grass, and do not categorise them as weeds, the difficulties they have surviving in my garden due to over-nutrition from nitrogen in the air makes it clear that my garden is not an island. The surrounding area has an influence on it, no matter how hard I try to shield it.

It is not just the birds who fly here and there that connect it with the other gardens in the neighbourhood. Or the bees, who carry nectar and pollen from the flowers in my garden to their hive and create new bees and honey with it. The garden is connected to the surrounding landscape and urban and agricultural atmospheres. This train of thought makes me reflective, since poisons are probably also brought in from the fields, not just the manure, whose smell goes right up your nose. Out there, no weeds have been allowed to grow, meaning that the insects, and with them the birds, have disappeared.

If a swallow ever flies over my garden, it's a real treat. The swifts that nest in the corners of some of the church towers in the town still glide directly over my garden, sometimes flying low when it rains. But for how long will the few insects that come from the gardens be enough to feed them, when gardens are becoming more and more uniform and manicured? I manage to attract sparrows with fat balls the whole year through, but they also need insects for their chicks. Is what they find here and in other gardens enough to raise a brood? The roughly fifteen sparrows who use the fat balls on a daily basis only bring a few fledglings with them. Will I also have to witness their slow but sure disappearance over the next few years, just as I did with the swifts? The term 'weed' covers more than the simple distinction between useful and not useful. In the near future, the number of plants we classify as 'weeds' and the number of plants we allow to grow will decide what kind of nature will surround us.

Trees and Shrubs

The majority of the trees and shrubs in my garden date back to the previous owner. They were a kind of dowry and, as sometimes happens with gifts, they were also a burden. I like many of them, but I would have never planted some of them. It wasn't their fault that they were there, and so I left them, almost all of them. I assumed that watching how they grew and thrived would show me what fitted well in the garden and what didn't. The species that were weaker would be simply overgrown, just like in nature.

Fortunately, I didn't make any predictions. Looking back, I am forced to realise that I would have got it all wrong. Bushes and trees are different to the flowers and vegetables that I plant and tend in order to harvest or delight in them. Since native and non-native species of trees and bushes have always been represented more or less equally in number in my garden, over the course of a decade I was able to learn what flourishes best under the conditions my garden can provide, and how they react to my care.

The garden was designed before easy-care conifers came into fashion. Back then, exotic diversity was clearly à la mode. I was surprised to find some Japanese plants: an aucuba and a Japanese beautyberry. I thought I would be accused of nostalgia for having these plants in my garden. However, it wasn't homesickness but rather their beauty that led me to keep them and actually to plant another Japanese variety: a star magnolia.

I have also been trying for several years to grow a common camellia outdoors. Also known as the Japanese rose, it was originally a house plant that bloomed such a magnificent red that I wanted to keep it. On frosty winter nights when ground temperatures are forecast to drop below minus five degrees Celsius, I protect it with a plastic covering placed over a cane dome. Thanks to two winters without any really hard frosts, it has not only survived but also provided a delightful abundance of beautiful flowers.

I have also planted bamboo: a large one that has grown to over three metres in height, and what was supposed to be a small one, which does not want to remain the dwarf bamboo I purchased it as and has sprouted shoots that reach chest height. With the exception of the flowers on the star magnolia in April, when the bush is shrouded in palm-sized white blossoms with star-shaped petals, my 'Japanese' plants do not push themselves into the foreground visually, nor are they prominent on account of their number.

The hedge is the largest feature in the garden. It was already here when we arrived, but over the last decade it has grown thicker and bigger. Two native species are dominant in the hedge: hornbeam and dogwood. The gaps that they leave are filled with native dog roses, yews, and privet, as well as the non-native but common garden shrubs of cherry laurel, forsythia, and mock orange. There is also a stretch of thuja hedge.

Together, they form a very dense thicket around the house but leave the side facing the street open. Rising from the hedge are thin, pyramid-shaped thuja towers alongside the double trunk of a birch, which is currently approximately ten metres high. There were originally three trunks, but one of them had grown so far over into the neighbour's property that we had to have it felled. Hornbeams can reach at least the height of the thuja, if not higher. They were originally planted as a trimmed hedge but are now shooting up, because although my husband trims their sides so that they do not overhang the pavement, he doesn't take anything off the top so that they provide the garden with privacy. They have long since fulfilled this purpose, excessively so. Birds, above all sparrows, are hornbeam advocates; they feel safe in their thick branches in both summer and winter, which is why we are often reluctant to carry out their overdue pruning.

I regard the hornbeams as even more of a marvel than the roses. The more they are cut back, the more they grow. Roses react with flowers in a never-ending succession from mid-May into the winter, while the hornbeams grow ever-thicker branches that hold on to their leaves throughout winter. Other bushes tolerate pruning far less well, or not even at all. Our rowans' growth has been stunted since we had to cut back a few branches because they were growing too far into the neighbour's garden. The thuja also reacted badly to a trim, and the side facing the garden now looks brown and dead. I hope that the wild grape vine will cover it.

The cherry laurel keeps growing and growing, even when I cut it back, and flowers fantastically although it produces very few cherries. The native yew has also become overgrown; its poison allegedly keeps competitors at a distance. My two old Japanese plants have been affected by it: the aucuba, with its gold-flecked, laurel-like leaves, and the Japanese beautyberry.

It is only in late summer that the beautyberry reveals the very unusual, shimmering, blue-violet pearls to which it owes its name. In Japanese, we call them *murasaki shikibu*. Murasaki Shikibu, or Lady Murasaki, after whom the berries are named, is the author of the novel *The Tale of*

Genji (written in around 1008). She is considered to be the world's first novelist. Even though they are hardy, these shrubs would not have survived in my garden without my energetic support.

The privet might be in danger of being squashed by the neighbouring native dogwood. I highly value both these shrubs because their berries, which are poisonous for humans, are eaten by birds, albeit with some hesitancy — apparently, blackbirds and thrushes don't find them particularly tasty. Northern waxwings gobble them up if they venture this far south in the winter. It is worth keeping the privet and the dogwood for these birds alone. The former can also provide food and shelter for privet hawk-moth caterpillars. That means that hummingbird-sized privet hawk-moths can also be found in our garden, which is another particularly compelling reason to tolerate the privet, despite its rather whiffy flowers and the fact that every part of it is poisonous to humans. That said, almost everything that isn't classed as a fruit or vegetable is poisonous to us.

The hibiscus shrubs were additions I made to the garden. As they are a hybrid form of the Asian perennial mallow, they flower in white, pink, light violet, and sometimes a mixture of all these colours. I prefer to refer to my hybrid as hibiscus, even though it doesn't look like the more common species that flowers blood red, originates from southern China, and is common in the South Pacific.

I think its delicately toned white, light-violet, or pink flowers are at least as beautiful, if not more so. At any rate, they are not quite as garish. The special connection I feel with my hibiscus plants is renewed in May and June, when I commence my battle against the aphids that attack them each year. I end up using so much nettle manure that I can no longer smell anything else. Then, in the summer, when they bloom all the more beautifully because of it, I feel as though my efforts have been worth it.

I do not need to put in as much effort with the hazel tree. It grew of its own accord, most likely because a jay hid a nut by the garden fence and forgot about it. I could not have planted it in a better location, so it was allowed to grow until it threatened to knock over the fence. Regrettably, an unplanned radical prune appeared to have killed it, meaning we weren't able to enjoy eating home-grown hazelnuts. However, shoots eventually started to grow out of the rootstock, and it became a bush — a very thick, very fast-growing bush with large, possibly record-breaking leaves. Some of them are as big as my whole hand.

After a few years, in late summer, it formed catkins that then unfolded on warm days in February and released clouds of pollen. I could see that it had also formed female flowers: little red tongues reaching out of a bud. The outcome was hazelnuts once again, and from year to year they grow in number. Nut-tree tussock moths, which live on the leaves of the hazelnut, have also returned, along with the hazelnut weevil, which uses its absurdly long, thin proboscis to bore into the hazelnuts.

I will not get to see its cousin, the acorn weevil, which pierces acorns in a very similar manner, in my garden. In my lifetime, the oak tree, which was almost certainly also planted by a jay and is now growing more or less in the centre of the lawn (surrounded by stones to protect it when we mow the grass), hasn't managed, even in the best conditions, to grow big enough to form acorns and attract acorn weevils and jays. I will have to satisfy myself by finding both these acorn eaters in the woods. Like so many other species, they make it clear again and again that they see no distinction between 'nature' and man-made habitats like my garden.

After a decade, I took stock of the plants in my garden. This revealed that the garden was home to around fifteen species of trees and shrubs that are native — in the broadest sense of the word. I say 'in the broadest sense' because the apple saplings have been cultivated and are not direct descendants of the central European crab apples. The vines are also not exactly native, but not being able to classify them properly doesn't bother me; I just love their grapes' divine taste. The roses are a borderline case. Their cultivars are descendants of a Middle Eastern rose species but cannot be traced back to either of the two roses that freely grow out in the wild here: the dog rose and the field rose.

I don't know how to classify the blackcurrants, either. In any case, their harvest, which varies from year to year, can be made into a wonderfully aromatic jam. We used to have a damson plum tree in our garden, but I can barely find any information on this species. Almost every year it produced vast amounts of round dark-red fruits that, when they fell, would be immediately covered with flies and wasps. As they began to ferment, they would attract admirals, peacocks, and other butterflies. The tree was positioned between the thuja and the birch, but a summer storm damaged it so badly we had to fell it. Sprouts from its roots never managed to grow properly, because the two large trees on either side of it shaded them too much.

The spindle tree, my last native addition to the garden, unfortunately isn't thriving. Its growth has been stunted and it is always being attacked by aphids. Most likely, it will not survive. It is proof that native soil is in no way a guarantee that species will thrive. It is not just my Japanese camellia that is hanging on for dear life.

The approximately fifteen natives are joined by twenty non-native species, which are all more or less thriving. The forsythia and the weigelia are naturally included in this group, and they are found everywhere in the garden. The weigelias produce large, red, trumpet-shaped flowers into which bees and bumbles dive until they disappear, and the forsythia's famous golden blooms adorn the bushes in March and April before its leaves sprout. However, despite its vibrant blooms, forsythia offers pollinators nothing. I am not sure how much, if any, joy my hibiscus offers bees, either. At least they can find some pollen and probably also nectar on the mock orange flowers. While the variety that grows in my garden unfortunately doesn't have a scent, it does still provide at least a little excitement for pollinators.

In May, before its few flowers open, it shoots up about a metre in height. This new growth feeds a shocking number of aphids. Combatting this infestation is far beyond what I am capable of. I would rather just get rid of the mock orange. This is why, every year, my husband cuts down and takes away all the new sprouts. It limits the infestation, but probably also the plant's flowering capabilities.

The remaining non-native species cause me no problems. The two red-leafed Japanese acers that I planted are growing splendidly. So much so that I really ought to learn the basics of bonsai if I want them to remain small and pretty and keep them from becoming large trees. I have no inhibitions when cutting back the forsythia or cherry laurel. Often it's other people's opinions that determine how these hedges look. Their crude and mundane leaves don't spark my interest. It's different with the Japanese acers; their delicate, palmate leaves hold a kind of symbolic power and mean a lot to me.

When I occasionally read or hear of the deep symbolism that German oak leaves once held, or when I see the maple leaf on the Canadian flag, I understand my feelings better. The deep-blood-red leaves of the Japanese acer are the autumnal equivalent of cherry blossom in spring for the Japanese. I collect the fallen leaves from my Japanese acer and display them for a while, enjoying their beautiful forms. On the lawn, they construct a work of art, until they are covered over by the small yellow triangles of the birch leaves, which rain to the ground on some autumn days after the first frosty nights of the year.

Of course, trees and shrubs shape my garden, just like they shape the majority of the gardens in the neighbourhood. Trees tower over everything, bushes form property boundaries, and greenery and flowers flourish almost the whole year through. Gardens create their own worlds with very rich and diverse ecosystems that offer wild animals and plants much more than they can get from the agriculturally exploited meadows that harbour only an extensive monotony of non-native plants. None of their crops are native — not the ever-so-common maize, nor the wheat. Not even the red poppies that survived a chemical cosh and have been able to flower. In those fields, beauty is not valued, and so I think it is all the more important to maintain beauty in my garden.

Birds demonstrate impressively that trying to cultivate beauty in a garden doesn't make it hostile to life. By visiting my garden, they cast judgement. Sparrows nesting in the thuja because they can no longer find anywhere to nest under sealed roofs find this tree as alien to them as human houses, but are still happy to make it their home.

When in the summer or early autumn I see butterflies, hoverflies, and bees on the buddleja flowers, it reaffirms my opinion that this is a plant that should continue to be grown in this country. The same people who argue that this bush should be combatted and exterminated complain that insects can no longer find flowers and that their numbers have declined steeply. Are the insects' own judgements not worth anything? Is the prejudicial distinction between 'native' and 'non-native' the only thing that matters? It does not seem to matter in the agriculture and forestry industries. They don't care about this question; they are only driven by profit. I don't have a guilty conscience about the species diversity in my garden, not even in regard to the flowers. I know that birds, butterflies, bees, and even, in their own way, aphids and other pests, are on my side.

III.

Harmony in the Zen Garden

As a child, I would often spend time on my own in my grandparents' tea rooms. The four small rooms could be entered from the garden from all four points of the compass, in accordance with tradition. I liked the little doors that led into the tea rooms because their height (sixty-six centimetres) and breadth (fifty-seven and a half centimetres) suited my diminutive child stature. I didn't think about what that meant for the adults who were forced to enter bent over on their knees. I also liked the simplicity of these rooms, which correlated to the four seasons and the corresponding different positions of the sun.

The rooms often only contained fresh flowers that my grandmother or grandfather had placed in an appropriate position. These arrangements captivated the eye and turned the emptiness into a room. On entering the tea room, a guest must bow to the flowers. I can no longer remember what I would do first after creeping in. Maybe I simply sank into a meditative state similarly to when entering a church whose sheer size and enclosed space demands contemplation. I could also have sung or recited a poem with much emotion but no audience. Or maybe I simply sat on the floor and embraced the silence. In any case, I felt happy. In retrospect, I am sure of that.

My grandparents' house was surrounded by a garden. That must have been a privilege, for even back then space was scarce in Japan; a garden was generally just a small appendage attached to a home. Here in Germany, front and back gardens are often so small that you can barely landscape them, and they generally back straight on to the neighbours'. I had the impression that in post-war Japan, a tea house in the garden would have been more cherished than the house itself. The time spent in my grandparents' tea house must have been formative, because every time I have set foot in a Zen garden since, it has taken my breath away. I sense a magic or hidden fascination being emitted from these 'typical Japanese gardens', as they would be described, and a meditative mood comes over me as soon as I enter one.

This feeling could be compared to the euphoria of reaching the summit of a mountain on your own or as a pair, without having to endure the chattering of a queue of mountain ramblers. This is the only way in which the magnitude of nature can be felt, and a meditative mood develop; its charisma unfolding through the silence. We Japanese often spontaneously bow our heads before a mountain and its magnitude. This haiku by Nichio Okada characterises our awe: 'I stand before the mountain, bow my head, and welcome the new year.'

The design of a Zen garden awakens this feeling of magnitude and eternity, despite the garden often being small in size. Such design is characterised by harmony, as I, a lover of classical music, like to put it. It can be enjoyed both in a simple room and in a grand concert hall because of its harmony. The skill in designing a Zen garden is in achieving such cohesion. It is not solely the visual aspects of the garden that determine its harmony. It is also one's own mental state within it, as well as the acoustics, which is ideally a silence that 'chimes' (as I once read). A mere description of this garden design is simply not enough. You have to experience it, enter into it, and feel the harmony with all your senses.

There are some elements that form the garden's frame and its essential content that are consistent from garden to garden, but as scenes, they are borrowed from nature, which is lively and ever changing. Geometric structures like rectangles, triangles, circles, or repetitive symmetry are alien to Zen gardens. Such shapes are characteristic of French parks, which are extensions of palaces, intended to show the absolute power their rulers hold over nature. In them, everything has to be subject to the absolute dominance of man's volition. Zen gardens are very different. They even make absolutist rulers such as the shogun and the emperor reflective, and offer them a release from their daily business.

The tea ceremony was originally intended for meditating monks to escape time, since a Zen garden opens up a gateway to nature. In a Zen garden, there are no exact lines and no straight paths, not even figurative 'life paths'. Rather, there are shapes that are connected to each other: trees, bushes, cliffs, rivers, moss, decay, lichen growing on hard stone, and flowing water. Shifting light and shadows complement each other. The green of the vegetation appears in all tones, from the vivid yellow of young leaves to the dark green of moss cushions in barely visible corners and angles. The designers of such gardens are not interested in symmetry but rather in a calming authenticity taken directly from nature and arranged simply, yet at the same time artistically.

This kind of artful gardening never reaches an end point, for nothing is ever considered complete; it is all a process. Everything has been thought of, even calculated, or predestined, yet is concealed from the visitor. Even the stepping stones, which are clearly intended to allow a flow of water to be crossed with moderate steps, or a bridge, which arches over a stream, hide their intention to direct people's feet in such a way as to be able to embrace nature. They are part of the arrangement, just like the rocks and the bushes, the winding paths, and the views. They all unfold. Maybe I can describe it as follows: it is nature, but a nature that conforms to humans.

Many Zen gardens, even very small ones, have their own way of removing limitations. They open up to the sky, to a future that approaches then lingers close by. When I set foot in them, daily life disappears as if it has been sucked into an invisible, dark hole. After a few moments, I feel changed, relieved, inspired, and deeply calm. Nature is no longer antithetical or even alien; it has become part of my world. It is not the wilderness — I didn't know of such a thing before I came to Europe — rather, it is life that accommodates, accepts, and almost absorbs me. It allows me to participate in the bigger picture. If a gong and its echo ring through a Japanese temple garden, it appears as if the sound has come from eternity, or rather from timelessness. The gong affects me as if I were meeting the master who made this garden into the very thing that I was experiencing.

When I am in this mood, I intuitively understand what Goethe meant with 'he makes the moment lasting'. At that, my heart overflows. The sensation of beauty can escalate into something painful, as I experienced during a lonely hour in the moss garden in Kyoto. The gleaming light of the sun was illuminating the midday hour in the garden, and I had sunk into contemplation of it without noticing. Suddenly a dark shadow was cast over it, and everything that had just been so bright was now plunged into shades of darkness that gained a physicality. What had appeared flat, as if drawn, became structured. As the shadows grew and grew, the moss lost its lustre. The scene, whose beauty had so deeply moved me, disappeared. I stood still and understood the meaning of vanishing and transience.

Where possible, a Zen garden is designed so that light and shade, as well as the course of the seasons, provide an understanding of the impermanence of beauty. It not only lies in the eye of the beholder, but also in moments of changing light. Harmony should be reflected in the selection and arrangement of the stones, in the layout and maintenance of the sand, in the cushions of moss, in the clumps of ferns, and particularly in the natural elegance with which the water flows, humming its own barely audible, delicate melody. Water should not be fired into the air from man-made fountains, forced to rise and fall, but it may trickle downwards as if choosing its own course.

Visitors from Europe or America would most likely assume that Japanese gardens resemble the Japanese landscape shrunk to the size of a garden, and that these gardens, featuring mountains, rocks, streams, and little rivers surrounded by green, as if by magic, represent a distant view of mountainous islands in the way bonsai shrinks real trees down to garden or room size and, in doing so, makes them manageable. That could well be the origin of why Zen gardens look as they do. It's common knowledge that it is difficult to observe your own culture objectively, with the necessary distance, if it's even possible at all. Someone creating a rockery in Germany will most likely have the Alps in mind as their inspiration and will select Alpine plants that thrive in lowlands (with suitable care) correspondingly.

However, at least in my experience and estimation, Zen gardens don't aim to shrink the natural landscape to garden size; they seek to do exactly the opposite, to open up an inner landscape of experience and unify it in greater harmony. In doing so, the garden is no longer an object, as I myself forfeit my isolated subjectivity. Maybe I can use this feeling to explain what I mean by 'Zen garden' and what it means for me.

A Zen garden is not a (small) paradise that shields me from the rough reality of its generally not-so-paradisiacal surroundings — although it does occasionally or even frequently fulfil this function. This aspect can be compared to the curation of home decor, which creates a sense of wellbeing and lets you feel 'at home'. In the living room, the 'self' doesn't unfurl into a bigger harmonic entity, even if you are extremely satisfied with the design. Breaking down the barrier put up by daily life requires external harmony. In Zen, the world opens up from within itself — it isn't illuminated from the outside. The power of nature expresses itself in this way. I have experienced this both in the wild nature of forests and on rivers, as well as in the contemplative silence of old graveyards that haven't fallen victim to the renewal and purging fads of our times. This feeling touched me as I was guided through the Japanese garden of Augsburg and was told the story of how it came to be.

However, the best way to find harmony is working in your own garden. Single glances can be enough, for instance at the Japanese acer with the round stones next to its trunk; at the gazebo, which is, after all, an echo of a tea house; or even at the stepping stones that lead to the gazebo. Such moments encourage an awareness of the flow of time.

Maybe this feeling is what Rainer Maria Rilke meant when he wrote, '*Jeder Tag ist der Anfang des Lebens. Jedes Leben der Anfang von Ewigkeit*' ('Every day is the start of life. Every life is the start of eternity'). Such words stand like cliffs against the flow of time and evanescence. I can only grasp them in the moments when I deliberately contemplate shadows cast by trees, drink in the colours of opened flowers, or watch grains of soil as they fall through my fingers back into the flower bed.

When drawing on this sense of mindfulness, my garden becomes a Zen garden, even though it was not designed or intended as such. I experience the thriving of the plants and the difficulties against which they struggle, for they are nature, and part of life in nature is constantly battling between growth and demise. That is precisely what the

Zen mindset teaches me, and it calms me. I enjoy the beauty and forms, the colours, and their diverse nuances, not to mention the quiet atmosphere that unavoidable neighbourhood noise cannot really affect — although I sometimes wish I couldn't hear cars passing on the street or lawnmowers in other gardens. In awe, I experience how external noise disturbance is lessened when I am deeply moved by the flowers of the morning glory, so luxuriant on summer mornings, or by the late roses in autumn or early winter. Such moments reveal how my senses interact much more than I was aware, especially when I want to be 'all ears' or 'all eyes'.

My observations in my own garden allow me to understand better the writings of the Japanese author Jun'ichirō Tanizaki in his lauded but controversial book published in 1933 as *In Praise of Shadows* in English. His view of Japanese aesthetics, which sought to preserve the shadowy past, is a mystery to me. I simply regard it as a critique of civilisation, since he so vehemently rejected electrical lighting and was of the opinion that Japanese living rooms should be kept in half-darkness in order to conform to his sense of beauty. Rooms would only be in half-darkness because it was unavoidable before electric lighting was introduced, not because the Japanese population desired it. The same goes for the Europeans for whom electric light provided a new brightness and the opportunity to do things in the evening, like reading.

What Tanizaki anticipated in his work *In Praise of Shadows* is today regarded by many as light pollution. Many complain about it in Germany: there is too much light, much too much of it, and it's everywhere, even where darkness would actually provide more illumination due to the full moon and starlit skies. I think about the garden in regard to this problem, and, as always, it helps illuminate my thoughts. It offers me fine colours and tones at various times of day, so I remember always to keep my eyes open to them.

I need not be seeing it in morning light, though it is wonderful to see the intensity of the colours increase with the height of the sun. The colours become more vivid, the shadows more pronounced, and the structure of everything increases. Of course, I am enraptured when the setting sun illuminates my garden with its golden light, when the acer leaves turn blood red, when the blinding white of freshly fallen snow creates a virtually new garden, or when, in the spring, the green in the garden is so soft that I am not sure if I should class it as green or as yellow.

The nuances are even more subtle on cloudy or dull days covered with autumnal mists, or if an approaching summer storm suddenly 'turns off' the light that had just been so bright. The fading light or afterglow can awaken a deep emotion in me, if I take the time to contemplate it. In good weather, I find the garden beautiful in all seasons. That in itself is not uplifting. It's altogether different when I feel

202

unexpected sensations that I had previously not noticed. They lead me into a state that I call outwardly directed meditation, in which beauty gains a different meaning. It is no longer subject to the customary comparisons; I embrace it as it is, in the way I experience it, not by judging it, as I usually do.

My simple garden, which has been somewhat left to nature, also allows me to summon relentlessly notions of enchantment. I hear the sounds of the silence, observe the interplay between grasses, bushes, and stones, and experience the flowing together of all my senses into that which I consider 'beautiful'.

The garden exhales the spirit of Zen while I inhale its atmosphere, as I like to put it. Its beauty is simultaneously infinite and very personal. For me, it is expressed by the four fundamental elements in Chinese: 和敬清寂. Insight, which cleanses the inner state, and thankful respect, from which harmony grows. This is how I experience Zen. I value it so highly as a life principle that in such moments I'm moved to tears; tears of gratitude in a state of happiness.

The things that left an impression on me in my childhood as I experienced my grandparents' garden and embraced the special importance of the tea house still have an effect on me, but they don't prescribe how my garden should be or how I want to experience it. When gardening, I am often distracted by the small events that are generally overlooked or disregarded. For example, when a hummingbird hawk-moth — which, unlike other hawk-moths, flies and visits flowers during the day — whizzes past me on its way to the buddleja. Does it recognise me as a harmless creature benevolent to its existence? Does it look at me as it hangs in the air before the flowers, wings whirring and straw-like proboscis sucking up nectar?

The peacock butterfly beside it pays no attention to me as long as I keep a distance of a metre or more. The bees, which visit the flowers by the dozen, don't consider me at all, even when I spend a while watching their industry. In a few minutes, tableaux of life fly past me; their abundance quickly becomes too much to grasp. I rest my eyes by looking at the leaves that have fallen from the Japanese acer and glancing at the roundness of the boulder next to it, or at the white birch bark with dark-grey fissures that entice you to look for patterns that mean nothing. I especially like the birch trunks; they were a background consideration when I was searching for a home and garden.

In the garden, I haven't hung any lanterns to remember my ancestors. However, many moments of conscious lingering are a suitable way to remember my parents. Here in the West, remembering your ancestors is often derogatively called 'ancestor worship'. However, this is a core element of Japanese Shintoism and is different in a positive sense from the communal remembrance on All Saints' Day in Germany, which feels rather strange to me. Often, formal rituals are and remain incomprehensible. I shall not even attempt to use elegant words to explain what I mean by 'outwardly directed meditation' or how to achieve Zen in the garden. The experiences I have described in this book are better placed to do so.

Grey November — Inhaling and Exhaling

The last red leaves have now fallen from the Japanese acer, and were it not for a few yellow and dusky-pink roses, the garden would now be devoid of any colour. At least that is how it feels. Of course, that's only an illusion, for the vibrant hues of summer and autumn have now given way to a plethora of subtle browns. They have their allure but are not alluring enough to make up for this season's short days, mists, and damp chills.

The lack of bright light bothers me, as it does many other people, too. They call it winter depression or SAD (seasonal affective disorder). It sounds genteel, almost too nice for the dismal state of affairs it describes. After the *Föhn*, the wind that causes headaches but also bestows the so-called 'Golden October', has blown through, a November depression — one that brings conditions best suited to putting everything off — seamlessly slots in. This is followed by flu season and the Christmas depression. Then, at last, it's winter, and the world brightens thanks to snow and longer days.

I find November weather particularly hard to cope with. In the almost subtropical south of Japan where I was born and grew up, we didn't have such weather. There was always enough wind blowing in from the sea to prevent mist from forming. The temperature was tolerable, even comfortable, compared to the oppressive heat of the summer. It was the destination for many migratory birds, in particular cranes from North-East Asia.

Conversely, in Germany, these birds leave us. The ones that remain in my garden are: 'our sparrows', which we feed throughout the year; some blackbirds (I am never sure whether they are the same ones who nested here in the summer or not); and a few great tits and blue tits. Our winter guest is a robin. Every winter one of them stays in the garden, and I try to offer it suitable food. Occasionally it sings, and when it treats me to a concert in November, I am particularly joyful. The wonderfully wistful song of a robin is an acoustic bright spot in the darkness of the season.

The robin encourages me to take some pleasure in the pastel-coloured tones of late autumn. This period is locally known in Bavaria as *toter Herbst*, which translates to 'dead autumn'. Its name is not only due to the days of remembrance that are accompanied by grave decoration and commemorations, but also because almost nothing stirs in nature. Every year we anticipate winter as a victory over late-autumn stagnancy.

I give the garden and myself a jolt. Fallen leaves are amassing, and in the pale light the golden-yellow triangles of the birch leaves are practically glowing. The more I pile them up in the hope that a hedgehog will hibernate in them, the more they shine. The leaves of the hazel tree have turned brown, dark brown, or a blackish grey-brown. It is only now that I realise how much they vary in size. Some are larger than my hand, while others only cover half of it.

When raking up the leaves, I notice that there are still flowers in the garden. Daisies poke their little heads slightly over the grass, now so thin that we no longer have to mow it, and rest on the moss. The daisies keep their buds closed and will only open them when the cloud cover breaks and the sun shines through. To my surprise, I also find some orange-red hawkweed. I am particularly fond of its reddish-gold petals.

When the brown leaves lay on the ground, I didn't notice these flowers, which no bee or any other insect will visit. They don't need pollinators because they fertilise themselves to form seeds. I find it fascinating. How else would they be able to flower in this season without insects and other pollinators? Dandelions, whose autumn flowers are the most visible, with their yolk-yellow petals and several-centimetres-long blooms, also self-fertilise.

Snowflakes have been known to fall on the spherical seed heads of dandelion clocks in December. Snow white upon silver grey. But it's only momentary; either the flakes melt or the dandelion clock is smothered by the snow. I also find some speedwell, with its tiny, sky blue, uncommonly delicate flowers.

All these little stimuli come together, and as I contemplate them, it becomes an exercise in meditation. I would like to describe it as a mindful admiration of nature. Zen is not always about carrying out strict exercises, encompassing the lotus position, *sesshin*, or answering complicated *koan* questions in order to gain enlightenment.[2] Immersion in nature is calming, and it reduces the pressure that builds up due to the lack of light. I am now able to embrace better the subtlety of the late-autumn colours. A thought materialises — maybe the golden days of October with their radiance would be too lurid, too unsuitable for this season.

A mosquito takes off; it had been sitting in the leaves that I am raking together. As if in slow motion, it flies over the garden at knee height for a few metres and settles again. In the afternoon, it dances with the others in what looks like a living column of smoke. It is actually the winter crane flies

2   *Sesshin* is a period of variable length in which a person commits themselves to a concentrated Zen meditation. It takes place in a Zen monastery or in a training centre, where a significantly more intensive *zazen* (seated meditation) is undertaken than in daily Zen practice.

rather than the mosquitoes that bite. How can such a delicate insect, which more or less consists of just two wings and six extremely thin legs, live at this time of year? And survive the winter? Despite the cold in February, in those first mild afternoons when the temperature is only a few degrees above zero, the crane fly will be on the wing again and shall dance in my garden. Their small bodies are thin wands just a few millimetres in length. Such a small life, yet so intense. It makes me ashamed of my initially dismal mood.

When I potter around and embrace all the small things still living in the garden, I become less demanding and more satisfied. Relaxed and without fear of what will happen soon or in the more distant future, I submit myself to the passage of time. Discarding fears is one of the central aims of Zen meditation. I learnt that from my father. We lived in a region where it was probably appropriate to have fears: fear of the Sakurajima volcano erupting (its name means 'cherry island', and it is the symbol of the city of Kagoshima, just as Mount Vesuvius is for Naples); fear of tsunamis, whose sudden force cannot be predicted; and fear of typhoons, whose arrival may well be predicted a few days in advance — but what use is that if your home is to be ripped apart and blown away?

I was surprised when I came to realise that even in Germany there is fear. There is even a fear of good weather in the summer, even though it is not good enough for the millions of central Europeans who flock to the

Mediterranean every year. Fears are spread by the media —
anything that changes in any way generates fear; all it needs
is for the change to be hyped. The first snowfall is reported
as if it were a catastrophe, yet not having a white Christmas
is treated in the same way. The Zen consciousness tells me
to embrace the day, the time, and the changes. Nothing can
stay as it is, nor can change come at the precise moment it
is desired. It would be a waste of energy to fight it. In the
garden, maintaining a Zen mindset helps me to embrace
change. All living things, whose life cycles I am slowly
becoming acquainted with, embrace whatever happens.

I sense this most clearly in the mornings when I
am picking flower stalks covered in glistening dew for
the *ikebana*. Through the soles of my feet, I can feel the
dampness of the earth, the gentle distinction between the
leaves upon which I tread, and the elasticity of the moss
that doesn't compress under me. It bears my weight as
if I were no burden. Before me, birch leaves glide to the
ground. The dew that has settled upon them is enough to
detach them from their branches: a tiny weight, but one
that nevertheless weighs.

Here and there a drop of water bursts on the ground.
I see the largest drops on the rose leaves, which are still
lush green, growing vigorously with waxy-smooth upper
sides. They will continue to feed the buds and bring them
to bloom in December. Then, contemplating the blood-
red, finger-like leaves of my small Japanese acer, the soft,

rhythmic music of Johann Sebastian Bach's 'Goldberg Variations', which suits the mood so well, flows through me. Canon to canon, it crescendos like the moist fog that begins to fall drop by drop, becoming a fog shower. In this mist, I hear new variations of Bach-like music. They create an expanded sense in my Zen Buddhism.

Once again, I learn that the journey is the destination. It isn't a distant destination; the destination is the few next steps, the steps I must take today in order to manage daily life. They lead forwards to serenity, or maybe they are heading towards a future destination I am not aware of. At best I can hope that it will be a good destination. Zen meditation tells me to embrace the moment, the hour, and the day, even if that means cleaning, cooking, or other work. They are not necessary evils that you just have to get done; they're components of life, equal to the growth and demise of plants in the garden, the bridge over winter, or the constant flux between genesis and demise. Maybe the hidden power of gardening can be found in these seemingly mundane things. Through trying to shape the garden with the aim of harvesting food, we interfere with the cycles of nature, but we also must submit to them.

I observe the changes in the colouring of the vines. They are large plants, too big for it all to turn yellow or brown at the same time. The green vanishes slowly, yellow hues then appear, and, before the final wilting, a new colour palette is created. I muse that a painter could use the vines for inspiration — I photograph the colour variations, for I cannot paint them myself. I touch the leaves, smell them, and in doing so recall when, in the early summer, I made vine leaves stuffed with rice from their delicate young foliage. I particularly value such moments of sensuality.

In the garden, I have a 'secret' corner where I can immerse myself in a contemplative peace. There, I focus my breathing, take on any position that allows for calm inhaling and exhaling, and try to leave all thoughts behind. After a few minutes, the muscles of my neck and back, which had been tensed from stooping, relax. Just as with autogenic training, peace comes of its own accord. The luminosity of the delicate late-autumn colours increases. I can see the processes that lead to the fading of the leaves' green and to the storage of the valuable energy in the tree trunks and roots, as if watching a film in my head.

As the green fades, the yellow becomes apparent and in turn changes to gold and brown until the leaves fall. I am aware that this imaginary film is a pictorial representation of invisible activity, but its series of images corresponds to the actual processes occurring within the trees. I understand some of the general science behind nature's processes, but sometimes cannot quite understand the specifics. In my opinion, I don't need to know such details. In my garden I'm only interested in my modest contribution to genesis and demise, and in caring for life. When I potter around in it, I don't regard what I do as work but rather as a vocation.

The fact that it makes me tired leads to a relaxing tea break, not an invoice for hours worked.

In autumn, when my gardening tasks force me to bend frequently and for a long time, I often lift my eyes to the sky and watch the buzzards sail over me on their journey south. The call of the geese also makes me tilt my head upwards. They're on their own journey, a different one to mine in the garden, which I am trying to prepare for the winter. Of course, I know that it doesn't need this preparation. The birch, the various shrubs, the grasses, the moss, and everything that grows in the garden because it was planted by me or was tolerated after self-seeding would also survive the winter without my care.

Well, not quite all of them — there are a couple of sensitive shrubs among their ranks that I have to protect against frost in good time. For example, the star magnolia and the blood-red flowering camellia, which both come from a warmer climate — from my homeland, which is why I want to keep them and see them flower again next year. I also want to protect other, hardier shrubs against competition from more vigorously growing species, which I prune back in favour of diversity.

It is a well-known fact that you are never 'finished' in the garden. The work goes on and on, although sometimes at a different pace. I stop, put my tools aside, and think again about how I am to proceed tomorrow, in a couple of days, or whenever the time is right. The garden dictates the pace, but not my work schedule. Such a work schedule would give me sleepless nights. I sleep well when I know that I have done what was possible and necessary that day, as opposed to looking at what is to be done tomorrow. That is more or less what I learnt from the writings of Dōgen (1200–1253). Embracing this attitude is already a form of basic meditation. By appreciating the rhythm of life, time stands still, even as it continues on without impediment. Trying to get ahead faster than the rhythm allows eats up time instead of saving it.

Admittedly, when I was at school this was all too philosophical for me. Writing it down appears foolhardy to me, most likely because I don't have the words to describe adequately my experience of growing and thriving in the spring and summer. These images, which I have absorbed and kept in my memory each year, are more important than the words that would record them. How can I explain how I communicate with the garden?

The cycle of the year holds a special importance to me, and I see my own life reflected in it. It cannot be fully understood by anyone else, even if the work they do in their garden is similar. My feelings remain private, and that is what makes them so valuable. They create connections, and sometimes I think I am captivated by the moment like a small child playing with the reins that were intended to keep it safe.

The work I do in the garden is tiny in comparison

to what it does itself. It breathes, works, thrives, and lets things wither. It never stops living, even when there is apparent calm and snow covers everything. In November the garden is like a butterfly that is 'resting' in a stationary chrysalis, but within it something fantastic is developing that will hatch when the time is right. The caterpillar will transform into a butterfly. New life, not comparable to the life that came before it, is forming. The winter can come, I think, after I have again raked together a couple of piles of autumn leaves.

As if poking fun at my chrysalis comparison, a butterfly flits through the late-autumn dusk. It is a winter moth, a male with wings searching for his wingless female. She will be sitting somewhere on a stalk like a misshapen caterpillar, waiting for her mate ... and for a new generation of winter moths.

The shadows, which change as the light becomes weaker, can make the atmosphere in the garden feel gloomy. I overcome it by paying attention to details and trying to penetrate their meaning. As a result, thoughts come to mind that I pushed away in the summer, saying I didn't have time for them.

Garden Gnomes

At the end of the seventies, just after I had arrived in Munich from Japan, I saw my first garden gnome. He was standing in a garden that was easily visible from the pavement. First, I noticed the long, pointy, somewhat bent, bright-red cone on his head. I realised it was a hat because underneath I found a rather aged-looking face on a small body. The hat was almost as tall as this small person, who was wearing a jacket that had been painted on to him. In one hand he held a lantern.

Initially, I thought the figure was a child's toy, yet it was placed in the flower bed in a way that looked deliberate. I cannot recollect any more details, but the strange character stuck in my mind; I kept spotting ones like it in other gardens. They would be standing at the entrance to the garden, next to a flowerpot of the same small size, or between the 'mountains' in a rockery. Sometimes, there were several of them; occasionally, a group. I discovered that they were garden gnomes, whose origins are found in the bygone world of fairy tales. Apparently, they were fired from clay and then painted very distinctively. It was later explained to me that the fairy tale in question was *Snow White and the Seven Dwarfs*.

I took note of the explanations but was still surprised that a lot of people furnished their gardens with such gnome

216

figures. I should say 'decorate', for that is clearly their purpose. Garden gnomes are garden decorations in the same way that figurines, vases, and souvenirs adorn living rooms. I didn't dare ask the gardens' owners what the meaning of the gnomes was. Most likely such a question would have been considered impolite. That I found them strange, very strange, would have been obvious from the expression on my face. Beauty is in the eye of the beholder, so the saying goes. There is no universal definition of beauty, or what is appropriate when it comes to the arrangement of flower beds, paths, bushes, and small trees in a garden. Fortunately. It allows for the creation of individual designs, instead of a uniform monotony of gardens that all look the same.

I couldn't ascribe garden gnomes to any particular type of garden based on appearance, frequency, or arrangement. They were simply there, or they were not. They were not religious symbols — I never saw anyone looking upon one with devotion or meditating in front of one. It would not have been that absurd for me, as I have seen people do this in front of *jizou* statues in Japan, which I think have a certain similarity to gnomes. These heavily caricatured figures of children made from natural stone are sometimes about the size of a garden gnome but can be much bigger. However, the *jizou*, who wear a red or white bib, are not found in private gardens. They are lined up in temple grounds or stand along the paths and in quiet corners. They are gravestones without any name or any identification,

217

because they are markers for children who died before or during birth, and are sometimes even dedicated to aborted babies. *Jizou*s are intended to remember developing humans who could not live. The stone figures symbolise how they will remain in the pre-life state.

Wooden *kokeshi* dolls symbolise transience. They are intended as mementos of a special journey, and you can buy them in large shops. The heads of these simple wooden figures are large like those of babies. *Kokeshi*s are usually displayed in your home or at your desk. The person who places them knows their meaning or the memory that is connected to them, but may choose not to share it.

I was informed that garden gnomes are not *jizou*s or *kokeshi*s. Their origin goes back to very small miners, who, in the Middle Ages, dug for gold and precious stones, taking lanterns with them into the shafts. During the day, they would sleep from when they left the mine until their next shift. In *Snow White*, a delicate young girl ends up taking shelter with some dwarfs who work as miners, who are kind to her after her stepmother attempted to kill her with a poisoned apple.

After I had heard this fairy tale, I understood the intent and purpose of the garden gnomes even less. Or maybe I understood something very different: the garden is a place to which you can retreat and create a small, very private world that can be populated with elves and gnomes at will. The idyllic small garden represented triumph over hard times, which many survived in an almost fairy-tale-like manner. Fifteen to twenty years after the end of World War II, in the sixties and seventies, garden gnome culture reached its high point, meaning that what I witnessed was its decline.

This idyll, including the gnomes, was derided or joked about. Yet, garden gnomes still stand at small garden ponds with their fishing rods, even though the fish pay them no attention. Occasionally, a kingfisher uses the figure as a perch from which it can fish. The garden gnome trend was followed by the garden pond trend. The ceramic frog in various more or less accomplished forms has replaced the little men. Alternatively, a metal figure stands at the waterside: for example, a raven dressed in full medieval armour that can open and close its beak. It is an expression of the need to 'display' something in the garden, a need from which my garden is not exempt.

There is a stone boulder in my garden, right next to the Japanese acer. Between the two star magnolias, there is a long birdbath that has been carved from granite. It is just big enough for three sparrows or one blackbird to bathe in or drink from if they are thirsty. Furthermore, natural stones of various sizes are placed around the garden. If the lawn is to be mowed, I have to pick them up and then reposition them again. I don't have a particular pattern or arrangement in mind. I think of the stones as simple decorations, with the emphasis on simple. They shouldn't be excessively noticeable, nor should they provide a structure for or shape the garden. I think that task is fulfilled much better by the trees, bushes, flowers, and everything else that grows and consequently changes.

In autumn, one or two dark, blood-red leaves fall from the Japanese acer on to the boulder. The way they fall shows me the meaning of coincidence. The leaf just happens to lie there by chance and shimmers in the fine morning dew. Later, if it is touched by the fading autumn sun, it looks like an ink drawing on the stone. I admire such coincidental composition, for it is both calming and inspiring at the same time. Words and expressions start to form themselves into a haiku. I dare not explain why I find that so beautiful. The palmate, blood-red leaf landed at an angle and remained there; it is perfect without symmetry or intent.

We value such coincidences in Japan. Objects, such as vases, contain small deviations from the perfect form, which is precisely what makes them unique. In the same way, each leaf on a Japanese acer is inimitable when I contemplate it in detail and compare it with others. I hardly ever manage to find two leaves that are absolutely identical. Nevertheless, their symmetry remains obvious. These deviations are not harmful, as they are not mistakes or defects, but rather additions that create individuality. Just like humans with their infinite variety of faces, which are emphasised and amplified with jewellery, clothing, or, simply, the use of different gestures. Is it not the case that more beauty can be found in delicate, subtle individuality than in the pomposity and external finery that sometimes just serves to conceal an individual?

I haven't placed any gnomes in my garden, and I probably never will. Not because I reject them; taste and opinions are too varied to pass judgement. The reason is that I cannot use them to express what I sense and feel, which is characterised by expressions of simplicity or by the 'mantle of plain'. The two Japanese terms *wabi* and *sabi* could perhaps explain what I mean.

Wabi is derived from the Japanese word for solitude or loneliness (which was originally understood literally); it means that an object should stand alone and not be overwhelmed by too many other things around it. *Sabi* is the patina that comes about with (dignified) ageing; not the quickly appearing rust on a poor material but, rather, graceful maturing. Both of them together create a tension between what stands alone, such as a flower accompanied by a blade of grass in an *ikebana* arrangement, and that which is well aged because it is good and durable.

Ink drawings and the *ikebana* art of flower arranging are expressions of them. The 'mantle of plain' describes the interlocking characters of *wabi* and *sabi*. When it is expressed, be it in the garden or in art, I am gripped by a feeling of spiritual desire for beauty. Zen Buddhism aims for *wabi* and *sabi* without prescribing how they should be. What they mean can only be intuitively grasped and not formally understood by critiquing art or devising a benchmark for it. Longer practice is required to develop an eye for it precisely because the uniqueness of the moment cannot be artificially brought about. I need the bitterness of lonely silence, freedom from prior expressions, and the calm that is necessary for every meditation. Anything opulent would either be a distraction or make it impossible to sink into contemplation.

Consequently, I think competitions as to whose garden is the most beautiful belong to a different realm. I need to dismantle a large, magnificent bouquet of flowers in order to reach the simple beauty of the flowers that have been brought together or, rather, forced together. They would never grow in nature in the same constellation as either the bouquet or the arrangement in the garden. For me, naturalness is worth more than abundance, and the uniqueness of an individual flower is more valuable than a lavish bouquet.

In my own garden, this sentiment brings me into conflict with the blooming flowers, which can sometimes be too much. For example, the roses, whose flowers I cut and place in vases around the house; or when, in only a few days, the forsythia becomes a spring fountain full of golden-yellow flowers: too many bloom at the same time. The peonies grow even bigger, becoming so heavy and abundant with flowers that they deprive me of their beauty. They tend to baffle me, rather than allowing me to enjoy their charm. I value the blooms of the morning glory and passion flower all the more because their buds open in succession over a period of weeks and months. As a result, each one on its own is a joy.

Pruning Trees

Having to prune trees hurts me at the best of times, but particularly in late autumn, when it is high time to cut back the hedge properly. Strangely, I am much less concerned about it in the summer, even though the branches, shoots, and tendrils that grow too far over the pavement are weighed down with green leaves, or — in the case of the climbing roses — are even in bloom. Since everything is flourishing so abundantly, what is pruned back is much less noticeable. If their branches are bare, then the pruning appears to go right to the heart of trees and shrubs, which in turn increases my reservations.

In order to justify my actions, I concoct an almost preposterous argument: the hornbeam, dogwood, dog rose, and cherry laurel are doing so well in my garden that they have become too rampant, and they are threatening to crowd out weaker plants. They have nearly managed to kill the beautyberry and its unique red-violet berries. They beleaguer the yew, despite it allegedly being able to defend itself against such competitors by emitting a poison. The rowans are now becoming thin and weedy, only able to grow skywards because they are so crowded, which means they won't bear many berries. Berries that the blackbirds and, when they come, the waxwings love as I do, that add colour to autumn and the grey of winter.

Even my apple trees lean forward towards the part of the garden open to the sky, because the hedge, which has long since grown above head height, steals too much of their light. During a spell of bad weather when they were in blossom, I took a paintbrush and pollinated the flowers by hand, carrying the pollen from one tree to the next because there were hardly any bees buzzing around their flowers. Were they in too much shade? Too hidden? Equipped with justifications from this train of thought, I pass judgement on what should be pruned back and to what extent. Nevertheless, it is still unpleasant.

I'm not sensitive. When gardening, I get scratches, cuts, splinters, and surface wounds. They heal. It's part of the process; no amount of dexterity can prevent injury. But cutting back whole branches or tree crowns that have grown over the course of the summer hurts in a different way. My scratches are like torn leaves or removed twigs, far from the heart of the tree or shrub. My skin protects my body as an outer layer; my hair is an anomaly that feels nothing when it is cut.

Recently, I have heard and read about plants having feelings, hidden and incomprehensible to us, or being able to feel pain; Peter Wohlleben discusses this in his books. Even if I cannot imagine plants having such feelings, I do wonder whether it matters to the tree that its crown is being cut off. Some trees cannot withstand it, such as spruces and firs. Yet, when I observe my trees' reaction to the late-autumn prune, I understand less than I would like, despite my best efforts and complete devotion to nature.

The hornbeam grows stronger and thicker the more it is cut. In jest, I might add that it uses its power of growth to show me my limits. I could only beat it if it were felled completely, but that is not something I ever will do or want to do. I want it to grow into a very thick hedge that can only be penetrated by small birds and functions as a living wall. Evidently, it would like to continue growing indefinitely towards the sky. In contrast, my rowan took the pruning so badly that it died when I chopped off a branch which I thought was growing in at an unsuitable angle from its side.

The dog roses behave differently as well, strangely, even. After the autumnal prune, they grow particularly long branches the next early summer, bringing forth a green fountain sprouting in all directions with barely any thorns. But they also don't develop any flowers. They do the opposite of my hybrid roses, which continue flowering into the start of winter, as if they were saying thank you for the pruning (what an absurd thought!). Once again, I am simultaneously bewildered and awestruck by the many different reactions to the same thing: pruning. Only one thing is clear: the trees and bushes would have grown differently without pruning, in their own particular ways.

My thoughts wander before the first branch is cut. A patchy memory from my childhood resurfaces, of being in my grandparents' garden. Our old gardener, whom as a child I saw as ancient, wiped sweat from his forehead with a thin towel he had slung over his shoulder. In the other hand he held tree loppers, and a pair of secateurs hung in the deep thigh pocket of his trousers. He was clearly undecided. The image disappears. Another begins to take shape. The gardener and my grandfather — or was it my great-grandfather? — are in the garden, drinking green tea from small, flat cups and smoking small-bowled pipes with long stems. They are looking at the trees. Musing, maybe talking. Or is one of them giving a mumbled monologue?

Then the gardener says, 'That is how we will do it!' He approaches the tree and prunes it, branch by branch, so quickly that I can only tell that branches have been cut when they fall to the ground. Shortly after, the tree has a new look. Or its previous look, which I can still remember. How it looked years ago, when it was even smaller and younger. It had never been regarded in isolation but rather as part of the arrangement of the garden, and beyond that as part of the landscape. The better integrated it was with the bigger picture, the more successful the tree maintenance in the garden was considered to be. Rarely could you find an individual tree standing alone, and rarely was any one tree's individuality allowed to be emphasised.

Even the high art of miniaturising nature to make bonsai trees has a tendency towards the stylised image of a tree rather than a unique shape. Pines should look like pines, even if they only grow to two or three hands high despite being decades old. In my own garden, I didn't contemplate including medium-sized bonsais suitable for a small garden. I wanted to allow the trees, whether standing on their own or growing in the hedge, as much individual growth as the conditions allowed. My garden did not become a 'Japanese garden'. That was never the intention.

Growth is at the heart of my garden. In addition, birds and other creatures should feel at home, even the cats from the neighbourhood who immediately retook possession of it after my dog died. With enough thick growth down on the ground, the birds should find adequate protection. It should also serve the mice, which we have sometimes watched clambering around to get at the sunflower hearts on the feeding station in what felt like the late evening, judging by the light, but was actually the late afternoon.

This way of thinking, which considers the further development of a tree and its integration within the garden, is certainly a part of the Zen approach of my ancestors and the people of their time. Am I any different to them if, before cutting back the hedge, I think of the robin and the wren? In their own way, these creatures are part of the arrangement, just like the shapes that pruned trees take on. Strangely, I don't know if there were many birds in my grandparents' garden. I can only remember the butterflies that flew about in it, and that I was often startled by fat caterpillars that munched on the leaves of the bushes.

I am sure that the caring gardener would not have allowed any tree or bush to die. The pruning had to be done in a way that meant the inevitable damage would be tolerable, and the tree would be able to overcome it. It was more than just a question of honour: it was an obligation for the master. And every gardener must be a master. For the true master, every action is done for the first time; it is never a formulaic repetition, for pruning and shaping interferes with the life of the garden. It's at these moments that I also feel particularly confronted with nature.

This approach teaches me calmness and security. Calmness because, through it, I understand the core principle of the Zen teaching influenced by Master Dōgen. Security because this Zen approach doesn't recognise a hierarchy of masters and is satisfied to strive repeatedly for perfection. In retrospect, I think I can see the essence of my grandparents' gardener shining through. He collected himself and his thoughts before he started his work. He used a kind of meditation to determine the start and course of his tasks and carried them out step by step, just as you progress through the Zen journey step by step. The gardener, even with his beginner's mindset, carried out his tasks like a master.

When pruning trees, I revert to a beginner's mindset. It is not the wealth of rules and rituals that direct me, but my state as a beginner. That keeps my mind open. It is what I find in front of me that directs my actions, rather than the expertise I have collected over the years. Besides, it is better that these experiences only subconsciously influence my course of action and do not lead me to set out goals.

So, sometimes I stand, perplexed, in front of a shrub, hesitating, or stopping completely because I have to recall what it looked like in the summer, and how I looked at it from the living-room window or from the patio. And then I imagine how it will appear after the prune, if I look at it with the eyes of a robin or our blackbirds. I think of how, in mid- to late summer, I delighted in the abundance of hibiscus flowers, but how in winter it is only a stopping point for the birds, where they can come to eat at the feeder or bathe in the birdbath. Next year the remaining branches shouldn't be so close together, in order to allow the flowers more space to open.

I wonder if, for the time being, I should leave the inward-growing climbers of the dog rose and only prune them in spring, as they offer the sparrows and the titmice ideal cover and opportunities to play. However, it is far easier to cut them now and pile up the branches and fallen leaves in a corner or two, so that hedgehogs can hibernate in them and robins have hiding places close to the ground. The more I learn of the hidden life in the garden, the harder it gets for me to decide my course of action concerning this network of connections and necessities. I understand all the more why Zen masters sent their pupils to work in the garden. The greats among them worked in this way and created further generations of masters. They learnt the essence of Zen through working in and with the garden, not through theories or particularly profound reasoning.

While working in the garden, the pupils experienced how natural it is for efforts to fail and how to deal with such failure. In many typical Western gardens, the person who creates them is considered to be a master from the outset, and all growing and thriving must follow their instruction. The garden and its care are based on more or less clear plans and, where possible, it should function like a well-oiled machine. From the Zen perspective, this approach is a constraint: a constraint that is inflicted on nature.

I think a person's style of garden maintenance is most obviously demonstrated through their late-autumn prune, for that is when things are pre-formed for the next gardening year. The prune creates the templates. My hedge, which runs round three sides of the garden, does not have such a blueprint. That is why the sparrows, the titmice, and even the robin like it so much.

That may sound like a justification as to why my garden has not been created according to a diagram and is not maintained according to fixed rules. Other people may think it has defects, but I explain that it is those 'defects' that actually make up a Zen garden, my Zen garden. I sense its magic in particular when, with the advancing dusk, it appears bigger and bigger. At that time, its disorder becomes the harmony of the not-fully-completed or of what has aged and matured over the course of time. *Wabi* and *sabi*.

It is incomplete because it is always in the process of becoming and changing. It is aged, yet not old, and one of a kind in its uniqueness. What more could I want? Does the shining golden eye of the toad, who hops through the garden looking for shelter in which to hibernate in the autumn, not tell me that my garden is a success?

With well-balanced and considered pruning, I prepare it for a new cycle, the passage of which will probably only be felt by humans. For the garden, it is a return. I would like us to get on well again — my garden, all its life, and me.

Epilogue

Gardening books mainly address plants: how to get a good harvest, how to make flowers bloom, how to display flowers, and how to make your garden a work of art with your own stamp on it. Although lettuce, tomatoes, potatoes, and other plants feature in my book, the focus is different. My garden does not have to produce. I coerce 'him' as little as possible. Maybe 'him' sounds a little too familiar, but that is how it should be understood. The garden is something akin to a partner: an exuberant being, influenced by my gardening, but not one I want to subjugate or fundamentally bend to my will.

The fruit that I harvest from my garden is good in every respect, because I don't use poisons or force growth by overusing fertiliser. In exchange, I also harvest relaxation and respite. Dining on home-grown potatoes is wonderful, but it is also magical to see the flight of the fireflies in the late dusk of a midsummer's evening. This experience is just as important for me as eating raspberries fresh off the bush or tasting my uncommonly aromatic blackcurrants.

In the beginning, I was simply delighted to discover each new living being as a co-inhabitant of the garden, yet over time I became aware that in the past, gardens must have been overflowing with creatures. It is shown through the names of many animals that frequently use 'garden' as a prefix: garden warbler, garden bumblebee, garden ground beetle, and numerous others. Other names use 'house': house sparrow and house spider, to mention but a couple. We should also not forget insects like the housefly, cellar woodlouse, and other wildlife that live in gardens and have also more or less conquered our homes.

Numerous species that predominantly or even chiefly live in gardens, such as the blackbird, don't have a corresponding signpost in their names but show through their behaviour how much this aspect of the human world means to them. It is illustrated by my experiences with blackbirds, which have affected me so deeply. So did the way my dog took ownership of the garden as his territory. He became an integrated garden inhabitant even though he was in the house at night. His presence benefitted the garden birds because he kept the cats out. On hot summer days, the blackbirds sank into the holes he dug in order to feel the earth's coolness. If he lay in the garden, all the birds would become animated and light-heartedly hop around. I want to follow his example. I would like all creatures that are capable of recognising it to know my harmlessness and learn that I am well meaning towards them.

Over the winter, fallen leaves and branches remain in a corner of the garden as a shelter for hibernating animals. The hedge is not pruned for the sake of its appearance, but rather is done in a way that offers birds protection and somewhere to build nests. We hung up nesting boxes, because in the foreseeable future neither the hedge nor trees would develop hollows that would be suitable for titmice and other birds reliant on them for nesting.

The lawn only looks like 'lawn' in the winter when the snow is two hands high and covers whatever remains of the thin blades of summer, which nevertheless bear seeds. As I mentioned before, it is mowed in a mosaic fashion to provide the best possible protection for the plants that happen to be in bloom at that time. It means that in late summer or autumn, fairy rings of fungus appear overnight in some spots. They create patterns that make me reflective and sometimes send me into a dream, and not just because the word 'fairy' is used to describe these mushroom circles.

In German they are called *Hexenringe*, or 'witch rings'. For me, the word 'witch' invokes the image of a wise old woman who could 'magically' use nature's poisons and stimulants as medicine, before this art was ousted by the magic of modern medicine. Although, some herbal remedies are still in use in Japan and East Asia, as well as in Europe.

Furthermore, these fairy rings demonstrate the invisible life hiding and working in the earth, and the processes of converting, destroying, and recycling that go on underground, allowing everything to disappear and rise again. These fairy rings make it clear that I understand nothing, absolutely nothing, of the processes that I can only smell when I pick up a handful of soil. The worm that wriggles from the earth is a symbol of this soil life: one that is large enough to be seen. Yet I understand the worm as little as I do the blackbird that eats it. The difference between me and the blackbird is that, despite being so devoted to the blackbirds, I return the worm to the realm of the earth. We and all living creatures are part of the fabric of life, which is sustained in cycles, and yet somehow, deep inside me, is the subconscious wish that all lives could continue without having to kill and eat others.

I was brought up with a Buddhist approach to life, and also with the contrary knowledge that this approach is not always possible in real life. Even if I eat a lot of vegetables, fruits, and other plant products, I am still eating something that once lived. The barrier that distinguishes us from all non-human creatures is not broken down just by eating meat specifically, but with every mouthful we take. It is from this that Zen Buddhism derives the principle of the righteous and responsible life, for instance responsibility for your own actions.

'Righteousness' in the sense of being correct and appropriate is achieved when we know we are part of a bigger picture and base our actions upon that. When I came to Europe, I discovered that the Zen Buddhist approach resembles the ethics of Immanuel Kant. And these ethics are just as difficult to translate into practice here as they are in East Asia. My plan was that the 'live and let live' maxim should at least apply in my garden. A couple of disappointments were inevitable; sometimes we fail even when we have the best of intentions — it is unavoidable. Yet this attitude also provides moments of joy that cannot be counted or measured.

The coming, the going, and the returning in the garden gave me the exhilarating feeling of swimming in the stream of time. The rhythm of the seasons repeatedly brought forth new things that surprised me or presented me with previously unknown challenges. While 'the sound of a falling leaf' could perhaps be a seasonal character for an autumnal haiku, the garden permeates my soul through a shower of yellow birch leaves dancing towards the ground and the downwards floating of blood-red leaves from a Japanese acer, or through late sunshine or an early frost. Through such moments and thousands of others, the garden satisfies my need to participate in life emotionally and physically, in a way that is mysterious, fascinating, and irreplaceable in equal measure.

Life does not take an orderly course but remains ordered. It comes into being from apparent chaos, for its reasons and background are not disclosed to us. Through the Zen approach, I embrace life as it is. The chaos I am confronted with becomes the spice. Year by year, I am in awe of how the garden emerges, how it forms on its own and enriches itself with life where I do nothing, and how it reacts to everything I do. Imperceptibly, it changes from day to day and, because of this, becomes visibly different month to month.

I sometimes wonder how the wren and the robin experience my garden. It inspires me to write a haiku. This type of short poem is meditation, for it follows a strict structure yet leaves every freedom to interpret and simply enjoy it through the words it contains ('the essence of Zen is expressed in poetry rather than in philosophy because it is closer to emotion than to intellect,' determined Daisetsu Teitaro Suzuki). The same could be said of the rose chafer that hurries to the rose flower, the peacock butterfly that drinks the nectar of the buddleja, or the small throng of winter crane flies that dance with their tiny mother-of-pearl wings in the faint winter afternoon sunlight. What would (my) garden be without this life and the amazing abundance that I experience there over and over again? My garden gives me so much because it is full of life. I want to give as much as possible back to this life.

Miki Sakamoto, December 2020

Acknowledgements

The Zen mindset expresses thanks through fellowship. It is difficult for me to capture this in words so I shall begin with something uplifting. It was and still is an immense joy to contribute my own haiku to the Hinoshima haiku society of my homeland. I would like to deeply thank my haiku teacher, Mr Makoto Maruyama, the main founder of this society. I greatly value his generosity in placing his magnificent calligraphies at my disposal. It was only through working on this book that I discovered how closely Zen is connected not only to gardening and nature but also to haiku poetry.

The idea for this book came from my literary agent, Dr Martin Brinkmann, to whom I send heartfelt thanks. An equally hearty thank you goes to the chief editor at Aufbau Verlag, Christian Koth, for embracing the idea, as well as his support and constant encouragement. He granted me the freedom to select and develop the topics I wrote about, which was amazing. Working on the book became a real pleasure. Concerning the translation into English, simple words of thanks cannot express how satisfied I am with the result. Catherine Venner has interpreted the meaning of my writing excellently. And working with Laura Ali from Scribe UK was a delight. Thank you so much!

Last but not least, I would like to dearly thank my husband, Josef H. Reichholf, for revealing and explaining the nature in the garden with all its small and sometimes large miracles. It is profoundly touching to be aware of them. The essence of Zen surely comes about through understanding.

With this book, I would like to commemorate my teacher, Japanese Indologist Prof. Hajime Nakamura (†). My parents accompanied me on long stretches of my life's journey. They acquainted me with Buddhism and Zen. How else could I thank them than with life itself?

Miki Sakamoto, December 2022

感謝

異国で、私が俳句を詠むことができますのは、故郷の **火の島** 俳句会のご指導のおかげでございます。また、その主宰者、丸山眞先生に揮毫を賜りましたことは、望外の幸せでございました。衷心から感謝申し上げます。俳句にとって禅が、禅にとっては庭と自然が、その心を表現できる道であることを、私は俳句に教えられています。

　カタリーナ・ヴェルナーさんは著者の意図をよくつかんで英訳してくださいました。ただ嬉しさと、満足感に私は満たされております。有難うございました。また出版にあたりスクライブ社のラウラ・アリ女史のご尽力に厚く感謝申し上げます。

　庭を主題に書くことを提案された文学博士マルティン・ブリンクマン氏、そして自由に書かせてくださった編集長のクリスチャン・コート氏の信頼に心からお礼を申し上げます。おかげで実に素晴らしい体験をさせていただきました。また、日常に見られる小さな不思議から壮大な現象にいたるまで、自然をつぶらに説明してくれた夫ヨゼフ・ライヒホルフに心から感謝しています。自然のその一齣一齣が実に鮮明に印象に残っています。

　また、インド哲学の大家、故中村元博士と父母のおかげで、仏教のみ教えに授かることができたことを追懐し、その出会いにふかく感謝しています。

令和二年十二月　阪本美紀

241

Literature

There are so many gardening books in the world that I would never have been able to read them all. Although whatever I selected to read was rich in information, sometimes I was confused by the instructions it gave, since my garden is apparently abnormal. I do not produce enough vegetables in it, I do not plant enough, and I allow wildflowers and wild plants too much space. I regard the literature listed below as an addition to the acknowledgements, because what I found in it pleased me and enriched my gardening knowledge. As this collection includes both German and Japanese books, I have listed them separately. I thank the authors in both languages in equal measure.

Borja, Erik: *Japanische Gärten. Gärten gestalten mit Zen*, Munich 2000.

Demski, Eva: *Gartengeschichten*, Berlin 2011.

Goulson, Dave: *Wildlife Gardening. Die Kunst, im eigenen Garten die Welt zu retten*, Munich 2019.

Hempel, Rose (postscript): *Zenga. Malerei des Zen-Buddhismus* (Paintings of Zen Buddhism) (Special exhibition at the Museum of East Asian Art), Cologne 1959.

Tanizaki, Jun'ichirō: *Lob des Schattens*, Zurich 2018.

Körber-Grohne, Udelgard: *Nutzpflanzen in Deutschland. Kulturgeschichte und Biologie*, Stuttgart 1994.

Okakura, Kakuzō: *Das Buch vom Tee*, Dusseldorf 2004.

Pearce, Fred: *Die neuen Wilden*, Munich 2016.

Pollan, Michael: *Meine zweite Natur. Vom Glück, ein Gärtner zu sein*, Munich 2014.

Ryosuke, Oohashi: *Die Philosophenweg in Kyoto*, Freiburg 2019.

Schmidt, Kurt R.: *Japanische Gärten*, Augsburg.

Schwarz, Stefan: *Der kleine Gartenversager. Vom Glück und Scheitern im Grünen*, Berlin 2019.

Suzuki, Shunryu: *Zen-Geist, Anfänger-Geist*, Bielefeld 1970.

'T Hart, Maarten: *Die grüne Hölle. Mein wunderbarer Garten und ich*, Munich 2018.

Zuckerman, Larry: *Die Geschichte der Kartoffel von den Anden bis zur Friteuse*, London 1998.

Japanese Publications

御所のお庭 (Garden in the Imperial Court), published by the Imperial Palace, Tokyo 2010.

Andou Toshio 安藤敏夫 園芸療法 (Therapy while Gardening), in 'Shininigaku' 森林医学, Tokyo 2009.

Fujii Eijirou 藤井英二郎 園芸療法と園芸福祉 (Horticultural Therapy and Horticultural Wellbeing) in 'Shininigaku' 森林医学, Tokyo 2006.

Inoue Shouichi 井上章一 寺と庭 (Temple and Garden) in
'The Japanese Gardens Kyoto', Tokyo 2007.

Nakamura Hajime 中村 元 仏教動物散策in 'Buddhist Beliefs
on the Animal Kingdom', Tokyo 1988.

Nakamura Hiroshi 中村 浩 .植物名の由来 (The Origin of Plant
Names), Tokyo 1998.

Nakamura Souichi 中村宗一 良寛の偈と正法眼蔵 (Zen Monk
Ryokan's Song of Praise for Buddha and the Holy Scripture
'Shōbōgenzō'), Tokyo 1984.

Shigemori Mitsuaki 重森三鈴の庭(The Garden of Shigemori Mirei)
in 'The Japanese Gardens Kyoto', Tokyo 2007.

Sugimoto Hidetarou (The Garden of the Poet in the Japanese Gardens
Kyoto), Tokyo 2007.

Suzuka Osamu 鈴鹿 紀 旅と植物(Travel and Plants), Tokyo 1996.

Suzuki Daisuke 鈴木大拙 日本的霊性 (Japanese Spirituality),
1944.

Uehara Iwao 上原 巌 森林アメニティー学 (Comfort through the
Forest, Forest Comfort), Tokyo 2017.

Yanagizawa Souen 柳沢宗淵　茶庭 (Garden for the Tea Ceremony),
Tokyo 1967.

Yusas Hiroshi 湯浅浩史 .植物と行事(Plants and Traditional Events),
Tokyo 1993.

By the same author and similar to this book:

Sakamoto, Miki: 'Gärten. Das Kunstvolle und das Natürliche:
Betrachtungen einer Japanerin' ('Gardens: The artistic and the
natural – observations of a Japanese woman'),
in Scheidewege 38 (2008/2009): 201–210.

Sakamoto, Miki: 'Poesie des Augenblicks in der Natur' ('Poetry of the
Moment in Nature'), in Scheidewege 45 (2015/16): 201–213.

Sakamoto, Miki: Eintauchen in den Wald 森林浴 (Immersing
Yourself in the Forest), Berlin 2019.

Index